School Transformation Through Teacher Appreciation

Kathleen Eckert

Copyright © 2022 Kathleen Eckert
All rights reserved.

ISBN 9798798238514

*To my husband Charles,
for always loving and supporting me.*

Contents

Part I: Transform
- **Chapter One: Trust and Empower Your Teachers** — 4
  - Let's Vote — 4
  - Faculty Meetings — 5
  - Let Them Decide — 6
  - Teacher End of Year Survey — 6
  - Pop-ins — 8
  - Professional Development Period — 9
  - Gift of Time — 12
  - Buy What They Ask For — 12
  - If You Don't Have the Money, Find It — 18
  - Given Them What They Ask For — 20
  - Allow Your Teachers to Teach Each Other — 21
  - Various Professional Development Opportunities — 22
- **Chapter Two: Instructional Leadership** — 23
  - Model Strategies/Guide Their Growth — 23
  - Share the Wealth — 26
- **Chapter Three: Initiatives** — 28
  - Houses — 28
  - Project Based Learning — 29
  - Essential Questions — 31
  - Teacher on Teacher Walkthroughs — 33
  - Teacher Video Reflections — 37
  - Data Room — 42
  - Technology Badging — 45
  - Give Them Voice — 53

- ☐ **Chapter Four: Utilize Your Community & Student Organizations** — 55
  - ☐ Donations — 55
  - ☐ Scavenger Hunt — 55
  - ☐ Step Contest — 58
  - ☐ Restaurants — 58
  - ☐ Insurance Companies — 58
  - ☐ Investment/Retirement Companies — 60
  - ☐ Real Estate Agents — 60
  - ☐ Student Organizations — 61

Part II: Momentum

- ☐ **Chapter Five: Support Your Teachers** — 64
  - ☐ Individual Teacher Meetings — 64
  - ☐ Professional Development Books — 65
  - ☐ Partner with Other Schools — 65
- ☐ **Chapter Six: Make It Fun** — 71
  - ☐ Bowling — 71
  - ☐ Altitude Trampoline Park — 71
  - ☐ Community Scavenger Hunt — 71
  - ☐ Goosechase — 72
  - ☐ Transformations — 73
  - ☐ Carnival — 74
  - ☐ HMS Olympics — 76
  - ☐ A/B Honor Roll Celebrations — 77
  - ☐ Fabulous February — 77
  - ☐ We Love October and We Love February — 78
  - ☐ Twitter Challenges — 81

Part III: Recognition

- ☐ **Chapter Seven: It's the Little Things That Matter Most** 84
  - ☐ Handwritten Personal Notes ... 84
  - ☐ Text Messages ... 85
  - ☐ Wristbands ... 86
  - ☐ Bright Spots ... 86
  - ☐ Hump Day Holla' ... 87
  - ☐ Candle of Learning ... 87
  - ☐ Teacher of the Month ... 90
  - ☐ Above and Beyond Award ... 92
  - ☐ Husky Heart Award ... 92
  - ☐ Jeans ... 93
  - ☐ Sweats ... 95
  - ☐ Hour Lunches ... 95
  - ☐ Staff Shout Out Board ... 96
  - ☐ Scratch Offs ... 97
  - ☐ Warm Fuzzies ... 99
  - ☐ Teacher Treats ... 102
  - ☐ Class Cover Thank You ... 102
- ☐ **Chapter Eight: Value Them as a Person** ... **103**
  - ☐ Staff Beginning of Year Google Form ... 103
  - ☐ Staff Notes for Me ... 103
  - ☐ Notecards Home ... 104
  - ☐ Teacher Appreciation Week ... 106
  - ☐ Teacher Appreciation Gifts
    - ☐ Something Nice ... 108
    - ☐ Thank You Book from Students ... 109
    - ☐ Letter From a Loved One ... 111
    - ☐ Bag of Notes ... 113
    - ☐ Student Videos ... 114

☐ Candy Bouquets	115
☐ What Wish Can I Grant For You?	115
☐ Staff Care Day	116
☐ Appreciation Time	116
☐ TAG Walkthroughs	118

☐ **Chapter Nine: Miscellaneous** — **119**

☐ Super Sonic Wednesday	119
☐ Funny Memes	119
☐ Baby Betting Pool	120
☐ Baby Betting Pool 2.0	122
☐ Easter Egg Hunt	123
☐ Easter Egg Hunt 2.0	124
☐ Mentor Thank You	125
☐ Chair Massages	126
☐ End of Year Ice Cream Social	126
☐ Shelton's Slide Show	126
☐ Fun Awards	127
☐ Twelve Days of Christmas	127
☐ Find the Penguin	131
☐ Convocation Shirts	131
☐ Get to Know Each Other Cards	132
☐ Reach Out to Parents for Help	132
☐ Secret Pal	133
☐ School Gift Certificate or Check	133
☐ Holiday Cards	134
☐ Team Building Activities During Professional Development	136
☐ Payday Breakfast	136
☐ Popcorn in the Teacher's Lounge	137

- ☐ Birthday Wall — 137
- ☐ Birthday Cakes — 139
- ☐ Snack on State Testing Days — 139
- ☐ Potluck — 139
- ☐ Chili & Soup Cook Off — 140
- ☐ Room Service — 140
- ☐ Root Beer Floats — 141
- ☐ Happy Cart — 142
- ☐ Tie in National Days — 143
- ☐ Wheel of Winning — 143
- ☐ Parking spots — 144
- ☐ Random Acts of Kindness Bingo — 144
- ☐ Justin Timberlake Video — 145
- ☐ King or Queen of the School — 147
- ☐ Find the Memes — 147

☐ **Chapter Ten: Don't Forget Your Substitutes** — 149
- ☐ Remind for Jeans and Special Days — 149
- ☐ Give Them a School Shirt for Jean Days — 149
- ☐ Sub of the Month — 149
- ☐ Super Sonic Free on Wednesday — 150
- ☐ Coffee Pods, Water, and Chocolate as They Check In — 150

☐ **Chapter Eleven: Other Ideas Not Used, Yet...** — 151
- ☐ Birthday Cards for Staff from Admin — 151
- ☐ Sunglasses with "Coming Soon" — 151
- ☐ Sugar Scrub — 151
- ☐ Infused Water — 152
- ☐ Holiday Stockings — 152
- ☐ Departments Take a Day of the 12 Days of Christmas — 152
- ☐ Popcorn Bar — 152

- ☐ **Chapter Twelve: COVID** — **153**
  - ☐ Happy Hour — 153
  - ☐ Goosechase — 153
  - ☐ Phone Calls — 154
  - ☐ Parades — 154
  - ☐ Appreciation Time — 154
  - ☐ Jib Jab — 154
  - ☐ Stress Bags — 155
  - ☐ M&Ms Heal Anything — 156
  - ☐ Teacher Appreciation Week Parent Email — 156
  - ☐ Trident Note — 159
- ☐ **Appendix - Initiatives Listed by Years** — **161**

School Transformation Through Teacher Appreciation

Introduction

It is vital to understand that a teacher's perception is their reality. Their perception will dramatically affect how they operate day to day and how they influence student learning. If a teacher authentically feels appreciated and loves their job, they will give you 110%. This will lead to growth, ownership, and satisfaction in the workplace and drastically impact your student achievement.

When I was a coach, I learned the importance of showing appreciation to those who played a vital support role for my program. This included the school secretary, the campus financial clerk, the paint crew who kept my softball field free of graffiti, the plumbers who worked on my sprinkler system, etc. Showing my appreciation for them in little ways and taking the time to chat with them when I saw them made them feel valued, and when I needed something, they were fast and always willing to help.

I always encouraged my fellow coaches to give their support people a cap or shirt from their program or just talk to them and ask them about their families. Unfortunately, they did not listen. Let me share a situation with you. If I had a sprinkler issue on my softball field I could actually text Mark, the district plumber, to give him a heads up. By the time my campus secretary would get the work order submitted my sprinklers were fixed and Mark would just mark the work order as completed. One time the baseball coach at my school had a sprinkler head that had broken, and he had a tournament coming up and needed it fixed. He had submitted a work order a few weeks before, but the plumber had not been out to fix it. The baseball coach knew I had a great relationship with Mark and asked me if I would help him. I sent Mark the following text: "I am sorry to bother you, but could I get a favor? Baseball has a tournament starting tomorrow and they have a leaking sprinkler head. Will you see if you can fix it for me?" When Mark came out to the field, I met him out there and chatted with him about his family while he fixed the sprinkler head. It took him about 15 minutes. The baseball coach was over there with us the whole time, but Mark never acknowledged him or even looked at him.

    I carried this lesson with me as I moved into administration. I continued to go out of my way to make people in supporting roles feel valued and appreciated, but I also began to think of ways I could do the same for my teachers. I knew if my teachers and staff felt valued and appreciated it would have a direct impact on the success of our students.

    After a few years I created a simple presentation for a conference titled, "Do Your Teachers Feel Appreciated?" The response I received was so amazing that it became my standard presentation for lots of different conferences. Each time I would update, tweak, and adjust my presentation based on the conference or new things I had tried on my campus. That presentation has now morphed into this book.

    This book answers the question, "How does one develop a campus culture where teachers and staff are invested in campus initiatives while feeling appreciated, valued, and supported?" By providing hundreds of ideas, discussing how some of the ideas came about, and suggesting ways to change or enhance ideas, educational leaders can easily develop their own plan to give their teachers the feeling of appreciation and therefore positively impact student success.

    A note of caution: You cannot implement everything in this book right away. You need to look at your campus needs and figure out what will work best for you and your campus. In other words, determine a starting point that will give you the most bang for your buck. Then slowly incorporate new ways to show your teachers how much you appreciate them.

    In this book I will divide the appreciation ideas into three categories: transform, momentum, and recognition. If you are like me and just want a list of appreciation strategies, you can implement quickly turn to Part 3: Recognition. If you want to use appreciation to push instruction initiatives start with Part 1: Transform.

Part I: Transform

Chapter One
Trust And Empower Your Teachers

One of the most, if not the most important thing we do as school leaders is hiring. We hire teachers because they are the experts in their content. You must treat them as such. Empower them to do what they need to do to help students master the standards and grow as individuals. Trust them to be the experts you hired.

Let's Vote

Why should you make all the decisions? On a regular basis school leaders must make decisions on a lot of little things. And to be honest, we are good with whatever the decision is on those little things. At the same time teachers and staff want to feel like they have a voice and a say in what happens, so periodically do brief surveys, and let them vote on what they want or what they think some of the decisions should be. These decisions can be small, medium, or large. The purpose is to let your teachers and staff be heard. Some ideas are:

- ☐ Extended lunches for the last week of school
- ☐ Home visit times
- ☐ Lunch options for meals provided for the staff on special occasions
- ☐ Recess

When you allow your teachers and staff to have a voice by voting, it is important that you share the outcomes of the voting with them. This means include the numbers or percentages with them as well as the decision. You will never have 100% of your staff vote the same way on something. By sharing the numbers or percentages those who voted differently will be less likely to get upset with the decision that was made.

Faculty Meetings

As a former coach I know from personal experience that it is hard to get to faculty meetings when they are before and after school. For the first faculty meeting I made it very clear that the expectation is that ALL staff members attend. I conducted six faculty meetings: before school, A lunch, B lunch, C lunch, D lunch, and after school. Then I put out a brief survey asking the staff if they would prefer future faculty meetings to be before and after school or during lunches. The entire staff voted to have faculty meetings during lunches. Let's face it, if you can take away a before or after school meeting teachers will rejoice.

The first year I gave teachers five minutes after the tardy bell to heat up their lunch. This left me 25 minutes for the faculty meeting. Meanwhile, people were calling my secretary and asking if they could speak to my staff at a faculty meeting. Eventually I put the two together and told my secretary to tell those wanting to talk to the staff that I would give them five minutes at a faculty meeting if they would provide lunch for the staff. Basically, instead of giving the teachers five minutes to heat up their lunches I was giving the person that provided lunch those five minutes to talk to the staff.

It was slow going at first. About every other faculty meeting we had lunch provided, and most of those wanting to provide lunch were financial advisors wanting to talk about retirement and such. Due to that, I did a survey with the staff at the end of the second year. I asked if they wanted to continue having lunches provided when possible or if they wanted to go back to having time to heat up their lunch and not have to listen to financial advisors. The staff overwhelmingly voted to continue to have lunch provided when possible.

As the years went on and more companies found out about what we were doing we were able to cut it down to the same two financial advisors coming each year and added in a variety of other companies such as banks, insurance companies, chiropractors, tax preparers, real estate agents, and fundraiser companies.

Who doesn't love a free lunch? By doing faculty meetings during lunches, we have taken away a before or after school meeting and by getting lunch provided, we are feeding them.

Let Them Decide

During the school year we have various campus professional development days where part of the days are also teacher prep days. (See Figure 1.1) Between October, December, January, and April I noticed that 14 hours was devoted to campus professional development according to the district spreadsheet and the rest was devoted to teacher prep time. As I was looking at the spreadsheet, I asked myself, "What campus professional development can I give my teachers in April that they will find beneficial and actually pay attention to?" So, I decided to juggle things around so that we got 14 hours of campus professional development in before April and the entire April day could be teacher prep time. I shared the two options at a faculty meeting and let the staff vote.

Truthfully, I wanted option B. But if I had just emailed out my revamped plan and said this is what we are going to do, a few teachers would have been upset. Allowing them to vote and then sharing the voting percentages made the teachers feel like they had a voice. It also kept the few who would have gotten upset from getting upset.

Teacher End of Year Survey

Conducting an end of year survey is a common practice. Most surveys have teachers rate things such as initiative, if they feel supported, if they are happy, etc. Think about this, if you do a survey and have your teachers rate on a scale of 1 to 5 if they feel supported and the average is a 4, how do you know

School Transformation Through Teacher Appreciation

Campus PD

Option A

- October 9
  - 8:00 – 9:00   Teacher Prep Time
  - 9:00 – 11:30   HMS Breakout Sessions
  - 11:30 – 12:30 Lunch
  - 12:30 – 2:00   YES Planning
  - 2:00 – 4:00   Teacher Prep Time
- December 15
  - 1:00 – 4:00   Teacher Prep Time
- January 3
  - 8:00 – 9:00   Teacher Prep Time
  - 9:00 – 11:30   RCA Breakout Sessions
  - 11:30 – 12:30 Lunch
  - 12:30 – 2:00   YES Planning
  - 2:00 – 4:00   Teacher Prep Time
- April 16
  - 8:00 – 10:00   Campus PD
  - 10:00 – 12:00 YES Planning
  - 12:00 – 1:00   Lunch
  - 1:00 – 4:00   Teacher Prep Time

Option B

- October 9
  - 8:00 – 11:00   HMS Breakout Sessions
  - 11:00 – 12:00 Lunch
  - 12:00 – 2:00   YES Planning
  - 2:30 – 4:00   Teacher Prep Time
- December 15
  - 1:00 – 2:00   YES Planning
  - 2:00 – 4:00   Teacher Prep Time
- January 3
  - 8:00 – 9:00   Teacher Prep Time
  - 9:00 – 11:30   RCA Breakout Sessions
  - 11:30 – 12:30 Lunch
  - 12:30 – 3:00   YES Planning
  - 3:00 – 4:00   Teacher Prep Time
- April 16
  - 8:00 – 4:00   Teacher Prep Time

Figure 1.1: Let Them Decide

Try open ended and anonymous surveys. Play with the verbiage of your questions to help with the feedback you get. For instance, when asking about an initiative, ask them what the strengths of the initiative are and what are some opportunities to help grow the initiative.

Every year I like to give the teachers and staff the opportunity to give constructive feedback to all administrators and counselors on the campus. Something I ask is, "What constructive feedback do you have for Mrs. Eckert?" I give each administrator and counselor their feedback the week after the teachers leave for the summer. At the beginning of each school year each administrator and counselor create three goals they want to work on that school year. I require one of their goals to be based on the constructive feedback from the teachers the previous year.

The first year I did this type of survey I tried to think of a way to help my administrators and counselors accept the constructive feedback, but also put the feedback in perspective if needed. I gave each person on the administrative team their feedback in spreadsheet format with the feedback I received in the second column. This way if they had something they felt was negative they could look at my feedback from that same person to maybe help them understand that person's perspective.

A word of caution: you need to have thick skin when you try this. The input can be invaluable, but some can also be hurtful. We all want to be liked by our staff, but in reality they will not always like you all of the time. It is in those times that you can use that input to grow as a leader.

Pop-ins

The first few years I did the Teacher End of Year Survey one thing I heard the most was for administrators to be more visible. Every year I brainstormed ideas with my administration team, but nothing ever seemed to truly work for us. In October 2017, a principal from another middle school in my district went to a conference and brought back the idea of Pop-ins and we quickly stole the idea.

Using the Class Dojo app, we set up five classes, one for each major hallway in our building. Then under each hallway we set each teacher up as a student. Each administrator was given access to the classes in Class Dojo.

From there all administrators started doing Pop-ins on a daily basis. When they Popped-in a classroom they simply marked it in Class Dojo.

Pop-ins are exactly as they sound. We simply opened the door and looked in the classroom. Sometimes we stayed a few minutes, but normally we went on to the next classroom. My administration team quickly turned Pop-ins into a competition. The administrator over our Class Dojo would put on the board in the teacher's lounge the total number of Pop-ins each administrator had completed and would update the board weekly. We started Pop-ins in January 2018, and by April we had been in over 3,000 classrooms. How awesome is that?

During the 2018-2019 school year, we put a spin on Pop-ins. During various administration meetings it seemed like there were a few teachers that were always at their desk when we went into or walked by their classrooms. We decided to use Pop-ins to gather data to determine if our perceptions were on point or not. So, we simply added in an "at desk" option. When I went into the app to click our name for a teacher's Pop-in, I could click on "Eckert" or "Eckert at Desk". This worked out great! It turned out that it just seemed like those few teachers were at their desks a lot, but in reality, they were not.

Professional Development Period

I have not met a campus principal or district level administrator that does not have the expectation of teachers planning together. In many cases the teachers plan before or after school about one day a week. That is simply not enough time if you want the planning time to have a true impact on student learning.

All the middle school principals in my district got together to work on a plan where core teachers would have two conferences. One conference would be utilized for department planning and the second would be the personal conference for the teacher. As a group we created a proposal and set up a meeting with our supervisor. After many meetings we were told we

TEACHER	CONTENT	PER. 1	PER. 2	PER. 3	PER. 4	PER. 5	PER. 6	PER. 7	PER. 8
McKethan, Stefan	ELA 7	Conference	Team 71	PAP ELA 7	PAP ELA (Con't)	ELA B	Advisory 7th	PAP ELA 7	PAP ELA (Con't)
New Teacher	ELA 7	Conference	Team 71	Advisory 7th	ELA A	ELA 7	ELA (Con't)	Mythology	Mythology
Morgan	ELA 7	Conference	Team 71	Creative Writing	ELA 7	ELA 7 (con't)	Advisory 7th	Cheer	Creative Writing
Beatty, Melanie	ELA 7	Conference	ELA A	Advisory 7th	Team 72	PAP ELA 7	PAP ELA (Con't)	PAP ELA 7	PAP ELA (Con't)
King, Brian	ELA 7	Conference	Advisory 8th	ELA B	Team 72	ELA 7	ELA (Con't)	ELA 7	ELA (Con't)
Chapman, Susan	ELA 7	Conference	ELA A	Advisory 7th	PAP ELA 7	PAP ELA (Con't)	Team 73	ELA 7	ELA (Con't)
Anderson, Jessica	ELA 7	Conference	Advisory 7th	ELA B	ELA 7	ELA (Con't)	Team 73	ELA 7	ELA (Con't)
Noland, Mitzi	ELA 7	Conference	PAP ELA 7th	PAP ELA (Con't)	ELA A	Advisory 7th	PAP ELA	PAP ELA (Con't)	Team 74
Mitchell, Stephan	ELA 7	Conference	ELA 7	ELA (Con't)	Advisory 7th	ELA B	ELA 7	ELA (Con't)	Team 74
Nevitt, Todd	ELA 8	Team 81	Conference	PAP ELA 8	PAP ELA 8	Advisory 8th	ELA 8	ELA 8	ELA 8
Morehead, Brandi	ELA 8	ELA 8	Conference	Team 82	Advisory 8th	PAP ELA 8	PAP ELA 8	ELA 8	ELA 8
Freeman, Heather	ELA 8	PAP ELA 8	Conference	AVID 7th	Advisory 8th	Team 83	ELA 8	AVID 7th	ELA 8
Pulis, Brittany	ELA 8	Athletics	Conference	ELA 8	ELA 8	PAP ELA 8	Advisory 8th	Team 84	Athletics
Davidson, Ashley	ELA 8	Athletics	Conference	ELA 8	ELA 8	Advisory 8th	ELA 8	Team 84	Athletics

Figure 1.2: Master Schedule

would get the extra staff needed to give all core content teachers two conference periods.

We had been dabbling with teaming at my campus. We currently had 2 teams for 7th grade and 2 teams for 8th grade for a campus of 1100 students. It was obvious we were not getting the bang for our buck with teaming for multiple reasons. The biggest reason was the number of students and teachers on each team. After meeting with leadership teams, we decided to move to 4 teams per grade level.

When we got the green light on two conference periods for core content teachers, I decided to merge it with wanting to revamp teaming. I locked myself away for a few hours and created a master schedule spreadsheet that gave all core content teachers one conference period with their department and one conference period with their team. (See Figure 1.2)

From there I created a Professional Development Calendar, (see Figure 1.3). On Monday, Wednesday, and Friday the teachers would meet by department and use their team time as their personal conference, and on Tuesday and Thursday the teachers would meet by team and use their department time as their personal conference.

February

Monday, Wednesday, & Friday - by Department
Tuesday & Thursday - by Team
Yellow - Electives Need to Attend

Sun	Mon	Tue	Wed	Thu	Fri	Sat
	1 TELPAS (Sims)	2 Husky Holla' (3)	3 Common Assessments & EQs	4 Team Meetings	5 Department Planning	6
7	8 Department Planning (ELM)	9 Department PD (Eckert)	10 Department Planning	11 Team Meetings & Data Posters	12 Department Planning	13
14	15 Staff Development	16 Husky Holla' (3)	17 Technology Harris	18 Team Meetings & Notecards	19 Department Planning	20
21	22 Husky Holla' (3)	23 CTE Meetings (L. Sheppard)	24 Department Planning	25 Team Meetings	26 Department Planning	27
28	29 Cornell Notes (AVID site team)					

Figure 1.3: Professional Development Calendar

In addition to department and team time, professional development was built into the calendar. Depending on what the professional development entailed or who the target audience was some professional development was done during department time and some was done during team time. Examples of the professional development included state assessment training for all staff, how to incorporate technology into lessons, instructional strategies, and much more.

Everyone has heard the saying, "if you build it they will come." This is very true for department common conference periods. Rather than taking it as a personal conference on team days, many departments ended up meeting and planning as a department during their department period.

Gift of Time

Everyone is always looking for time. With the implementation of our professional development calendar, we began to periodically give the teachers the "gift of time." This meant that they did not have a meeting or training for that day, so the teachers got both conferences that day to use as they would like. Now to be completely honest, I had fought pretty hard for the additional conference period for my teachers, and we had LOTS of room for growth and improvement as a campus. With this in mind I normally only give about two gifts of time a year on the PD calendar.

Buy What They Ask For

Each year campuses get a budget to use for "running" the campus. How are you using that money? Do you use ALL of the money you are given, or do you leave money on the table at the end of each year?

You will always have expenses such as subs, paper, copies, office supplies, and such that campuses need to use their budget money on, but how is some of that money being used for teachers and instruction? Most teachers do not ask their principals for things they need for their classroom. Somewhere in time, someone deemed those types of things a teacher's expense since they make so much money. :) If you hire teachers as the experts in their content, why would you not help them enhance their expertise and buy them what they need to do so?

Let's look at my 7th grade ELA team and their Engaged Learning Model (PBL) they created called Hero's Journey. The first two years of this project the teachers really focused on the guts of the unit and making sure they were properly leveling the state standards. Once they felt they got the leveling where they wanted it, they decided to focus on the launch of the project. (Keep in mind at the time I had eight teachers in that department.) I received the following email from my department chair:

School Transformation Through Teacher Appreciation

Sooo...

We have a really cool idea for our Hero's Journey Launch!!! Students are going to go on their own journey on launch day, complete, and compete various Hero's tasks in each of the English teachers classrooms. Students will earn house points along the way for each task they complete successfully. Some of the tasks will be content related, but other's will not. Which leads me to my request, we will be needing materials and supplies to pull this off. We are sending you our pie in the sky wish list for supplies and décor. Our launch date is set for Feb 28, so ideally we would need these things at least a week beforehand to set up.

We are well aware that we might be told no to some of it, but we are still going to ask. :)

The request included copies of various books for students, costumes for the teachers, materials needed to transform their classroom, etc. The requested amount was about $1500. I took a deep breath and said, "let's do it."

On the day of the launch the students started in their ELA classroom and watched a three-minute video that gave them directions for the day. After the video each student was given a card that listed the locations of the possible journeys they could choose from. Figures 1.4 – 1.11 are pictures of my amazing ELA teachers and their classrooms depicting various hero journeys.

As I talked to students in the hallway while they were going to the various rooms, they were excited and having a blast learning about the different heroes and their journeys. Seeing the enjoyment on both the student's and teacher's faces that day affirmed that the $1500 was money well spent.

Note: In this type of unit the launch is designed as the hook or to get the students excited. The next two weeks the students spent time learning about various heroes and their journeys. The students ended the unit by writing about their personal hero's journey.

Figure 1.4: Mrs. Stroope as Hermione at Hogwarts.

Figure 1.5: Mrs. Noland as Guinevere in Camelot.

School Transformation Through Teacher Appreciation

Figure 1.6: Mrs. Nelson as the White Witch from Narnia.

Figure 1.7: Mrs. Beatty as Dory from Finding Nemo.

Figure 1.8: Mrs. Anderson as Peter Pan in Sherwood Forest.

Figure 1.9: Ms. Lewis as Alice in Wonderland.

School Transformation Through Teacher Appreciation

Figure 1.10: Mrs. George as Maleficent in her moor.

Figure 1.11: Mrs. McKethan as Belle from Beauty and the Beast.

If You Don't Have the Money, Find It

I just shared with you one instance where the teachers asked for something and I was able to use school funds to get what they requested. But let's face it, there are times that teachers ask for things and we don't have the money. Reasons will vary from you are simply out of money or it is just too expensive. In those situations, you need to support your teachers by working to find the money. There are many ways you can go about this. Allow me to share three instances where I sought money to help give you some ideas.

Hillwood Middle School was named a National Schools to Watch and some of us attended the conference in Washington DC. While there, a few of us attended a session by McCracken Middle School from South Carolina. They presented on a program they call YES, or Year End Studies. In a nutshell, the last week of school all of the teachers and students spend the week doing community service. During the presentation one of my teachers turned and looked at me and said, "We need to do that."

McCracken graciously shared everything they had with us but seeing something of this magnitude in action would help us better understand "how" to replicate it. I had a group of six teachers who wanted to go spend a few days at McCracken during their week of YES in order to help us better plan for our own week of YES. I estimated that with airfare, hotel, rental car, and food this endeavor would cost approximately $6000.

I contacted the Keller Chamber of Commerce and shared with them my hopes of raising the $6000 and why. They graciously allowed me time at a couple of their monthly lunches to present our plan to local businesses in hopes of raising money. After those meetings and lots of meetings with the business members, we raised $4000. At that point the Keller Chamber of Commerce graciously gave us a scholarship for the remaining $2000. This reinforced that the businesses surrounding our school are always willing to help if you simply ask.

My second example starts with Kim Blann, the Director of Fine Arts for our district. She partnered with the Hudson Foundation to send

School Transformation Through Teacher Appreciation

representatives from an intermediate and middle school campus to the Ron Clark Academy to build a partnership between the two campuses using strategies from RCA. The initial group brought back lots of good stuff. As we began to incorporate strategies, we learned more staff wanted to visit RCA. I told teachers if they wanted to go, they had to set up a Donors Choose for the registration fees, at the time it was $900 a person, and if they got funded, I would pay the travel costs of airfare and hotel. The first year eight teachers signed up for Donors Choose. They posted their link on their personal social media and included it in their weekly parent emails. After a few weeks I then began an all-out push to all of our parents. I began posting on the school's social media as well as emailing all of the school's parents for help. In my emails I assured parents no donation was too small. After a few more weeks all of the teachers were funded.

I share this because if a school simply asks parents for help and explains the why behind it, the parents will step up. We also used this same process when Kerri Harris, our amazing campus librarian, wanted new tables in the library. She had the standard heavy tables that were part of the library when the school was built. Kerri wanted tables that were on wheels and could easily be moved around as well as tables that had the look and feel of a more modern library. The tables she picked out and created a Donor Choose for were about $5000. After Kerri, some of the teachers, and myself did a huge and constant push the tables were funded.

My third example started when I came to Hillwood. The campus had four carts of what were called netbooks (small laptops). The district I had just left had been a one to one district for three years. Let's just say I was shocked to only have four computer carts for 1100 students. Immediately, I made friends with everyone in the district technology department. Keep in mind this was before Chromebooks. At that time the cost of a laptop cart with 30 laptops in it was $25,552. Yes, that amount stuck with me. My entire campus budget at that time was about $100,000 for the year. I began the begging process. Technology found four iPod carts in the warehouse that were empty and collecting dust. I took those and spent about $3000 a cart to get 30 iPods per cart. The next few years I began to hodgepodge technology and take anything I could get.

One thing I did was invite the district's Director of Technology, Joe Griffin, to come walk the campus with me. I intentionally took him into the few classrooms that were using the netbooks and iPods. During our walk we discussed ways teachers were using what technology we had as well as what we could do if we had more technology. From then on, Joe often thought of Hillwood when he had money left at the end of the year or if he had some new technology, he wanted teachers to try out.

Fast forward a few years. Our mixture of technology had grown, but the netbooks were old and now outdated and the first iPods would no longer accept pushouts and updates. My supervisor at the time was always telling principals to let him know if they needed anything. To be honest, most people do not take advantage of these types of comments because they figure it is just a comment. Well, I typed up a nice proposal with quotes and all that fun stuff and set up a meeting with him. Chromebooks were a thing by now, so my quotes were to replace all of our old technology with Chromebooks as well as add more technology to the classrooms. The total proposal was about $100,000. I put my pretty proposal in a pretty report cover and set up a meeting. About a week after the meeting, I received an email from his secretary letting me know everything has been ordered. To say I was floored would be putting it mildly. But it did teach me that I need to ask. Think about it this way: if you ask the worst thing that can happen is you are told no and you are simply right where you started.

Give Them What They Ask For

In the last section I shared that my first year as a principal I had moved from a one-to-one campus to a campus with little or no technology. As I began observing and trying to decide where to start, I reached out to a friend who worked in instructional technology in a neighboring school district. Barry Fox had been an assistant principal with me at my former campus. I collaborated with him and set up a day for him to come out to Hillwood. Barry showed various apps to our teachers: Blendspace, Educreation, Doceri, etc. The apps he showed us could be used on the iPods we had or on student phones. The first year he came out and spent an hour working with teachers. The second year he came out for a full day and shared with departments. It has been several years since Barry came to Hillwood, but my teachers are still using some of the things Barry shared with us.

Allow Your Teachers Teach Each Other

Take a moment to stop and look at your teachers. Each one of them are truly amazing and they all have fantastic ideas. Capitalize on that by doing your own mini conference at your school on a professional development day. The first time I tried this I told all of my department chairs that I needed two session proposals submitted per department. To submit a session the teachers simply filled out a Google Form with the session name and a brief description of what the session would be about. Our sessions are 30 minutes each and we run four to six sessions at a time. I have found that doing what we call "breakout sessions" for 2-3 hours is perfect. It is an amazing way for your teachers to share their knowledge with their fellow teachers and it is a great way for teachers to add to their bag of tricks.

The first time we tried this there were two sessions that were mandatory, and those sessions were offered repeatedly during the 2-3 hours. This allowed me to get the teachers information I needed all of them to have while still allowing them to have a choice of some sessions.

During the 2019-2020 school year we took this idea a step further and combined with the intermediate school that feeds us. Teachers from both campuses presented and attended sessions and it was a great way for both campuses to learn about and from each other.

Tip: When you share the breakout sessions with your teachers so they can choose what they want to attend, leave off the presenter's names. This will nudge your teachers towards attending sessions that interest them instead of sessions their friends are running.

Various Professional Development Opportunities

All principals get emails about various PD opportunities. Share those you think have potential or line up with your vision with your teachers and see if anyone wants to go. You will always have a few who jump at the opportunity.

I like to follow-up with the teacher(s) after the PD to see what they learned or got out of it and see if there is something they could share with the staff.

Chapter Two
Instructional Leadership

Instructional leaders need to look at their teachers as if they are their students and the school is their classroom. Just as administrators expect teachers to differentiate, administrators must differentiate for their teachers.

Model Strategies/Guide Their Growth

All principals were once teachers. A great way to stay in touch with your teaching roots is to model instructional strategies for your teachers. Take the time to look at the needs of the campus and find fun, engaging strategies that your teachers can easily turn around and use in their classroom with their students.

Faculty meetings are normally times administrators simply impart information to the teachers. You will never be able to get away from this, but how you impart that information can be transformative. Think of the teachers as your students. What instructional strategies can you utilize in the faculty meeting to impart what you need the teachers to know? By taking the time to incorporate and model instructional strategies your teachers can use in their classroom, you are able to transform your faculty meetings into learning sessions, even if you are simply disseminating information to them.

One of my favorite strategies to model for secondary teachers are centers. Elementary teachers are masters at using centers in their classroom, but secondary teachers tend not to be. When I model this strategy, I like to create three to four stations. Put the directions for each station in the center of the table along with any needed supplies and mix up the types of activities at each station. Some examples are:

☐ Read the directions and complete the task outlined

- ☐ Watch a video (This can simply be the administrator making a video for the teachers to watch)
- ☐ Collaboration activity
- ☐ Gathering input from the staff
- ☐ Administrator led station

After the teachers have rotated to all of the stations give them each a notecard to use as an exit ticket. On the notecard ask them to write how they could use stations in their classroom. Type up the list and distribute the list to the teachers.

Technology offers lots of great strategies or tools, but you cannot model technology for the sake of modeling technology. What you model must be able to easily be carried over into the classroom by the teacher. Some great tools are Nearpod, Flipgrid, Plickers, Gimkit, Screencastify, and many more.

As I entered my second year of modeling instructional strategies for my staff, I began to put more thought and research into the strategies I modeled. By taking the time to incorporate and model instructional strategies your teachers can use in their classroom you are able to transform your faculty meetings into learning sessions, even if you are simply disseminating information to them.

For example, I read an article about hashtag summaries. I let the idea stew around in my mind for a few weeks. As my next faculty meeting was approaching, I went to NewsELA and printed out two articles. I print the Science article on green paper and the Social Studies article on yellow paper. At my faculty meeting I went over the items I needed to disseminate to the staff. Then I told them to partner up. One partner needed a green sheet and the other a yellow sheet. I told them to read their article and create a hashtag summary for each paragraph of their article. Once they finished reading their article, I had them tell their partner about their article by explaining the hashtags they chose for each paragraph. At the end of the activity both partners knew what each article was about.

Another time I had a reading strategy that our district English coordinator had shown me that I thought would be great for my English,

School Transformation Through Teacher Appreciation

Science and Social Studies teachers. So, I spent a few hours on the internet looking for a strategy I could share with my math teachers. I came across something called 3 Act Math. As I dove in, I knew I was onto something my teachers could utilize. Before I went too far into it, I contacted our district Math coordinator and ran the idea by her. Unknown to me she had been researching it and thought it would be perfect.

One more illustration is from when I was part of Principal Institute Cohort 6 from N2Learning. At the institute, Roz Keck had us read an article. Then we were each given six index cards. We were told to write our names on the back of each card and circle it. Then on the front of each card we were to write a statement from the article that spoke to us, for a total of six statements. Next, we were instructed to get up and go talk to six different people. We were to discuss our cards with them. They would take the card from us that spoke the most to them, write their name on the back of it, and keep it. Then they would discuss their cards and we would do the same process. Afterwards we should each have six cards: five that were ours and one that was theirs. Then we were to go do the same process with six other people. After we all went back to our seats. Then Roz asked who had a card with 6 names on it. If someone had one, they were asked to read it and tell why they chose that card. Next, they were to read the name that was circled on the back. That indicates the original owner of the card, and they were to say why they wrote down that statement. I loved this strategy and made a note of it.

Several months later I was meeting with a group of teachers to plan home visits to 550 students' homes the first day teachers return from summer break. I remembered this strategy and looked to find a good article about the impact of home visits. The day the teachers came back I used this strategy with an article on home visits. After the activity I did not have to discuss or explain "why" we were doing home visits. The teachers broke into their groups and simply got started.

About a month later I was walking by an English classroom and students were using this same strategy with their article of the week.

As you visit classrooms, look for strategies you can model. One of the biggest compliments you can give a teacher is to model to the staff something you saw in their classroom. When you do so, make sure you give the teacher full credit.

If you see a good strategy, make a note of it. It may be a few years before you think of "how" to use it, or it may be a few weeks. In the end a good instructional strategy is simply that. My favorite thing about modeling instructional strategies for my teachers is seeing them use them with their students. When I see this, I know I made a difference.

Share the Wealth

I have what I call a Teacher Involvement list. This list has the various initiatives with which staff members are involved with the planning and facilitating of each initiative. At the beginning of each year, I update the list. Then I compare it to the staff list and create a list of teachers not involved in something. When I look at playing with something new, I try to pull at least one person from the "not involved" list.

For example, when I decided to look at doing home visits for all of our incoming 7th graders (600 students), I pulled three teachers from the not involved list and matched them up with an assistant principal. One very influential teacher and two first year teachers. I met with them and shared my idea and a few articles about home visits I had found. They decided to roll with the idea. They had a planning day in May. At our end of year ice cream social, they showed a quick video to the staff and talked to them very briefly about the plan to visit 7th grader's homes in August. Then they planned another day in the summer to create the direction sheets, gift bags for the students, school informational sheets, determine which staff member is in each group, and the student list for each group. On the teachers first day back in August they presented the plan to the staff. Then the staff had 4 hours to do their 20-30 home visits and eat lunch. After that we met at the trampoline park for two hours and played as a staff. Many teachers came up to me that day and the next and said that was their best first day back to school ever. This goes to show that with the proper support, you don't have to go to your "go to" person for everything.

    Asking teachers to be a part of something can make teachers feel valued and special. Even if you have a negative teacher, you can word it just right to make them feel they are a vital part of the staff or the group/initiative you want them to be a part of.

Kathleen Eckert

Chapter Three
Initiatives

We all know that when you start a new initiative you need to have staff and teacher buy-in. This chapter is not about getting teacher buy-in. It is about how you can appreciate and/or incentivize your teachers so they want to be a part of and/or push initiatives. The fear of missing out can be a powerful motivator.

Houses

After visiting the Ron Clark Academy in 2014, Parkwood Hill Intermediate (PHI) and Hillwood Middle School (HMS) worked on a plan to start putting our students into houses. PHI has 5th and 6th grade students. It is across the street from and feeds HMS that has 7th and 8th grade students. Together the campuses created 8 houses that the students and staff would be sorted into. The idea was to house students in 5th grade, and they would remain in that house through 8th grade. Then during the school year teachers from both campuses would give students house points as rewards for various things and the winning house would go on a celebration field trip.

As with many things you do, if you incentivize your teachers they will work for the incentives and at the same time help with the success of what you are trying to do. For houses we incorporated the following incentives:

- ☐ House Point Wizard: A local restaurant contacted me and wanted to give us a gift card each month for the teacher of the month and in return they wanted us to post on our school website and social media about it. We already had a process for teacher of the month based on student nominations, so I decided to utilize this opportunity to incentivize teachers to give house points to students. The teacher who gave out the

- ☐ Scratch-offs: As part of the plan to incentivize teachers for giving house points each month for the House Point Wizard, we did five random drawings from those who gave house points during that month and gave them scratch-offs. (See Chapter 7: Scratch Offs)
- ☐ House Point Challenge: A few times a year I would offer a House Point Challenge where if teachers give out a set number of house points within a two-week period they can spin our Wheel of Winning for a chance to win prizes. (See Chapter 9: Winning Wheel)
- ☐ Color Out Days: Twice a month we have Color Out Days where teachers could wear jeans with their house shirts.

Project Based Learning

When Project Based Learning (PBL) was first becoming a thing I had a few teachers approach me and see if I knew of any training they could attend. Ironically, a few months later our district asked principals if they had anyone interested in learning about PBL. When I shared with my staff, those teachers, along with a few others, eagerly volunteered for the training.

The PBL training was called Engage to Learn Model (ELM). I attended the training with my five teachers. In all honesty, the training was brutal. The trainer kept shutting down the ideas my teachers had for lessons. I eventually pulled my teachers aside and said, "I don't care what the trainer says. I love your ideas. Run with them." In reality, when the teachers actually implement the lesson, the trainer would be nowhere around. You could visibly see the relief in their faces.

After the five teachers completed ELM training the district gave each of them ten Chromebooks. Chromebooks were relatively new at this time and we had very little technology on our campus.

Kathleen Eckert

At the end of the first year several teachers took notice of the Chromebooks the five teachers were given for ELM. When the district sent out information about the next round of training, approximately 15-20 more core content teachers volunteered to go to the week-long training in the summer before the second year. Then in December of the second year, the district came to our campus to train a few teachers who were late hires, but their department was wanting to do whole department lessons. I emailed the staff to see if anyone else was interested. Approximately 10-12 teachers attended the training.

This was around the same time that I submitted the proposal for technology to the district, (See Chapter 1: If You Don't Have the Money Find It). I was able to get Chromebooks for all of the teachers who attended ELM training.

As we began looking to year three of ELM, I had one core teacher who had not gone to the training. I sat down with that teacher and told him, "It is time for you to go to the training." So began our first year of whole campus ELM. Prior to the start of the year an assistant principal, the librarian, and a teacher were trained by the district as campus coaches. Since we would be whole campus the district saw the need for us to have the support on our campus.

As we started year four, we had an ELM coach in each grade level department. This means there was a coach in 7th English, 8th English, etc. The focus of the teachers this year was pushed to make sure you are aligning with the standards and leveling your DIY with less emphasis on the end project/product.

7th ELA was planning to launch their Hero's Journey ELM they had done the previous two years. They came to us with what they called their pie in the sky wish list. I looked at the amount, took a deep, calming breath, and said, "you got it." They were floored that I was going to buy teacher costumes, room décor, games, etc, (See Chapter 1: Buy Them What They Ask For). I had seen them implement this PBL lesson the past two years. Year one was a learning/stumbling block for them. Year two they tweaked and tightened up the lesson. So, year three they deserved whatever they wanted to continue to evolve the lesson. After the launch day I asked the department chair to debrief with her teachers and have them create a list of what they wished they had thought of to get before the launch, then get me that list and let me go ahead and get those items for the following year. This way it was fresh on their minds. And of course, if they come to me with more next year, I will gladly buy it for them.

Essential Questions

In Part 1 I encouraged you to share professional development opportunities you hear about that line up with your vision or plan for your campus with your teachers. Several years ago, I received an email about Essential Questions training. It piqued my interest, so I sent it out to the staff to see if anyone wanted to attend. Six teachers from various contents replied that they would like to attend.

The training was a two-day training and allowed time for collaboration. Our team decided that they wanted to develop a plan for all teachers to use essential questions and to have them posted on their board. Over the next few months, the team played with writing and using essential questions in their classes and using what they learned to create their plan for training the staff.

During our first full year of using EQs we added an area to our administrative walkthroughs for the administrator to type in the EQ posted on the board. Then at the end of the school year the team that went to the training looked at the list of EQs teachers used in their classes and realized they were actually low-level questions. Due to that, the team created an inquiry level for EQs and the following August they trained the teachers on creating EQs that are at level 3 or 4 on the inquiry level they created. The inquiry levels at the bottom of were created, (See Figure 3.1).

After our second year the EQ team surveyed the staff and based on their input we moved to what we call EQs & DQs. The Essential Questions are overarching for a unit and the Driving Question is specific to what is being covered in class that day. As the committee came to that decision, they also decided they wanted a way to give teachers suggestions and feedback on their EQ/DQ, how it connects, and how it is being used. That discussion brought about the other questions in Figure 3.1.

I am including our EQ to EQ/DQ process to show you what can happen if you offer professional development to staff and empower them to use the training to enhance student achievement. When this team of teachers met, I was in the room, but I took a back seat role to any decisions being made. This initiative was created, shared, and adjusted each year by the teachers who volunteered to go to the initial training. When you give teachers this type of trust and influence, they will flourish.

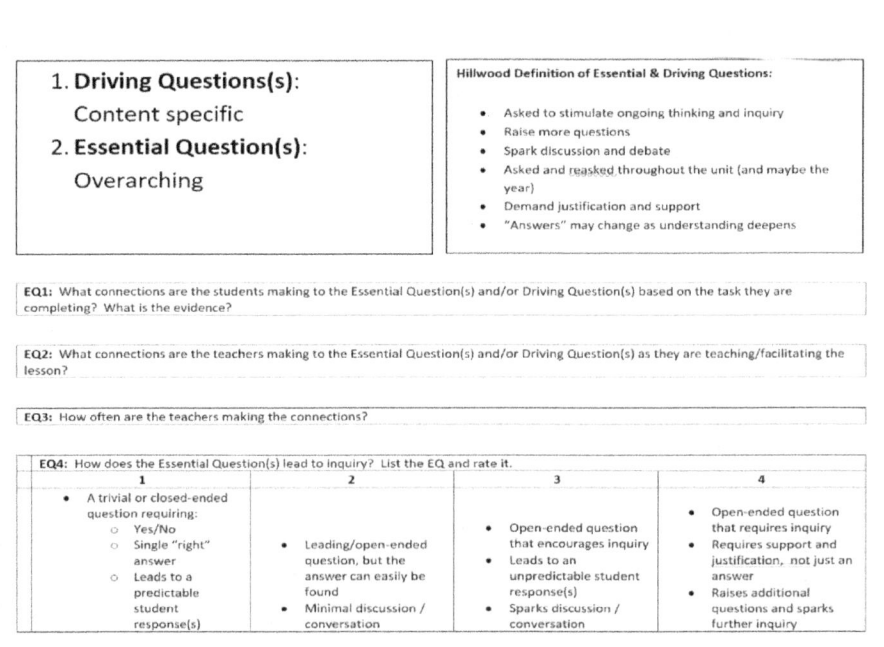

1. **Driving Questions(s)**: Content specific 2. **Essential Question(s)**: Overarching	**Hillwood Definition of Essential & Driving Questions:** • Asked to stimulate ongoing thinking and inquiry • Raise more questions • Spark discussion and debate • Asked and reasked throughout the unit (and maybe the year) • Demand justification and support • "Answers" may change as understanding deepens

EQ1: What connections are the students making to the Essential Question(s) and/or Driving Question(s) based on the task they are completing? What is the evidence?

EQ2: What connections are the teachers making to the Essential Question(s) and/or Driving Question(s) as they are teaching/facilitating the lesson?

EQ3: How often are the teachers making the connections?

EQ4: How does the Essential Question(s) lead to inquiry? List the EQ and rate it.

1	2	3	4
• A trivial or closed-ended question requiring: ○ Yes/No ○ Single "right" answer ○ Leads to a predictable student response(s)	• Leading/open-ended question, but the answer can easily be found • Minimal discussion / conversation	• Open-ended question that encourages inquiry • Leads to an unpredictable student response(s) • Sparks discussion / conversation	• Open-ended question that requires inquiry • Requires support and justification, not just an answer • Raises additional questions and sparks further inquiry

Figure 3.1: Essential Questions & Driving Questions

School Transformation Through Teacher Appreciation

This has turned into standard, expected practice at our school. Each August we do a quick, about 15-minute, refresher for our returning staff and a more in depth training for our new staff.

Staff buy-in for an initiative developed and adjusted in this way is almost seamless. You will always have those few naysayers, but by tweaking and adjusting the initiative based on staff feedback is a huge help to bringing them around.

Tip: If you have a naysayer on your campus you are concerned about, there are two possible options to help. First, if you have a strong group going to the initial training and you know the training is something you want to put in place at your school, talk to your naysayer and have them go to the initial training. This will put them as part of the team that creates and implements the initiative. This will give them ownership in the initiative. A second suggestion would be to invite them to join the team after the first or second year. If they are not interested in joining the team, find a nice way to tell them if they don't want to help fix what they feel is wrong then they need to keep their opinions to themselves. :)

Teacher on Teacher Walkthroughs

When I first started open ended surveys with the staff the most predominant request from teachers was more feedback. Administrators are pulled in many directions and work to get into as many classrooms as they can, but it is simply not enough. When I visited Smithfield Middle School in the spring, the principal shared with me their teacher-on-teacher walkthroughs. As I listened to the principal talk, I knew if we tried this it would be a great way to give teachers more feedback.

I took the idea back to my department chairs and they worked with their teachers on "what" they wanted feedback on. Each teacher created their form. On the top of the page was what the department as a whole wanted feedback on and on the bottom of the page was what that individual teacher wanted feedback on. I had clear sleeves hung up inside each classroom door and the teachers put their forms there.

During a meeting with my department chairs I told them we need to have a name for this process. One teacher suggested Husky Holla' and so it was named.

Once we worked out the plan, I discussed the Husky Holla' process at the next faculty meeting. At that time my teachers only had one conference period. I told my staff that teacher on teacher walkthroughs were optional and voluntary, but if they completed three during a week, they could wear jeans on the following Monday. I did not want to be the tracker of this, so we simply decided to use the honor system. As we got started only a handful of teachers chose to do this, but the impact was immediately evident. Let me give you an example. Approximately two weeks into trying Magen Rabatin, an 8th grade US History teacher, stopped me one morning and shared with me that Stefanie McKethan, a 7th grade English teacher, did a Husky Holla' on her first period class and suggested a website for her to try with her lesson. Magen had her second period students try the website and it was amazing. At this point not all of the teachers were bought in, but we knew we were moving in the right direction.

We knew from the school we took this idea from that at first the feedback would not be as constructive as we would like, meaning teachers would simply put "great" or "good job" and not give specifics as to why it was great or give ideas on how to improve. As we began to look towards the next year, we wanted to incorporate feedback training for our teachers.

The following school year we were given the PD period for core content teachers. So as we were gearing up to take Husky Holla's to the next level, we made them part of the monthly PD calendar, (See Figure 1.3). That meant we could build in days for Husky Holla's and require all core teachers to do them. That year we had three days a month on the PD calendar for Husky Holla'. Teachers were told that they could go during either of their conference periods and simply use the other conference period for themselves. For instance, if it was a department day on the PD calendar but the teacher wanted to see a teacher from their department, they could do their Husky Holla' during their team period that day and use their department period as their personal conference.

After our first full year of implementations, we discussed the pros and cons of Husky Holla' at our summer leadership meeting. The department chairs said they loved the feedback, but it gets hard looking for different things in different classrooms. They decided they wanted one form that could be used for any class you visit. They came up with the following areas for feedback:

- ☐ What I liked:
- ☐ Opportunities:
- ☐ How can I use what I saw:

The three questions were put into a Google Form and a QR code was placed by the door for each classroom. The teacher scanned the QR code, selected which teacher they are visiting, type in their comments, and hit submit. Then Google emailed the teacher who did the Husky Holla' a PDF of what they said as well as emailed the teacher they visited a PDF.

Essential Questions had been a focus for our campus a few years at this point, so a few months into the school year someone suggested we add a fourth area for feedback: Did you observe the EQ/DQ driving instruction? If so, how? (See Figure 3.1)

In the spring of our third year of doing Husky Holla' we hosted a workshop for teachers and administrators to come to our campus and see what we are doing in hopes of them taking something back to their campus. As part of the workshop, we had visiting educators do Husky Holla's and look for things we had talked about in the workshop. This allowed the visitors to see our Husky Holla' process and form while giving our teachers feedback from an outside source.

At the end of year four teachers asked to reduce the number of Husky Holla's they did each month. It was becoming obvious that many teachers began looking at Husky Holla' as something you "had" to do. So, leading into year 5 we reduced the number of Husky Holla' days per month on the PD calendar to two and planned to periodically remind the teachers of the why behind Husky Holla'. Don't get me wrong here. I fully saw the benefit of Husky Holla', but I also knew the benefit of listening to my teachers. My hope was that by reducing the number each month and with the periodic reminders of "why" the teachers would also see the benefit.

During our summer leadership meeting after the fourth year, we were discussing teacher feedback on Husky Holla' when one of the department chairs said, "I think it is time for us to evolve it." The teacher went on to explain that sometimes when he did a Husky Holla' if he saw a student in the room that he was trying to build a relationship with he would get sidetracked with that student and not get his other Husky Holla' complete. So, ICE (Investigating Classroom Excellence) was born.

With ICE teachers had two QR codes to choose from inside each classroom door. Under one code it said Student Advocacy and under the other it said Teacher Observation. If the teacher scanned Student Advocacy, it would take them to a Google Form that asked the following questions:

- ☐ Student Name
- ☐ What is one thing you noticed the student doing well?
- ☐ What is one area of frustration for this student?
- ☐ What behaviors does this student demonstrate in class?
- ☐ What additional support or strategies does this student need in place in order to be successful?

When the teacher submitted the form both the teacher completing the form and the teacher whose class it was were emailed a copy of the form. The thought behind the advocate part was to help both teachers possibly gain more insight to a student and to work towards building a relationship with that student.

If the teacher scanned Teacher Observation QR code it would take them to a Google Form with the same questions from Husky Holla':

- ☐ What I liked:
- ☐ Opportunities:
- ☐ How can I use what I saw:

☐ Did you observe the EQ/DQ driving instruction? If so, how? When the teacher submitted the form both the teacher completing the form and the teacher whose class, they observed were emailed a copy of the form.

In this book I share various initiatives with you that slowly evolved into something better based on teacher input and collaboration. With teacher-on-teacher walkthroughs we did evolve them into something better, but in this case, we actually went too far the other direction. When we added in the choice of teacher observation or student advocate we steered off of the original intended course. So, as we started our fifth year, I made the executive decision to take off the student advocate portion so that ICE was simply teachers giving teachers feedback on their classes. I share this with you because it is important to give your teacher's voice and make sure you listen. But when it is time to make an executive decision, you are the campus administrator, and you need to do what is best for your campus.

Teacher Video Reflections

If you have never videoed yourself teaching, leading PD, or interviewing you need to. It can be very eye opening to see yourself as well as to see how your audience responds to you. With this thought in mind, in 2014-2015, we started our journey of videoing teachers teaching. That year we had our assessment coordinator record each teacher using their iPad. The plan was to record all teachers during the first semester. The staff member created a schedule and shared it with the staff so the teachers would know when their lesson would be recorded. We used the teacher's iPad to give the teachers the secure feeling that administration would not be watching their video. Teachers were given a set of reflective questions to think about while they watched their video:

☐ Was the instructional objective met?
☐ Were the students actively engaged? How do I know?
☐ What went well? Why?
☐ What didn't go well? Why?

- [ ] What would you change?
- [ ] Was there an Ah-ha moment? If so, what was it?

The teachers were assured numerous times that they were not expected to turn these questions in or to discuss these questions with anyone. They were simply to help them reflect as they watched their video.

During the planning stages of this, I knew I was going to have foot surgery and needed to be off my feet as much as possible between the Thanksgiving and Winter breaks. Due to that I decided to meet individually with each staff member. (See Chapter 5: Individual Teacher Meetings) At those meetings the final question I asked each teacher was the only question that I asked them about their videoed lesson, "Were there any Ah-has that you would like to share with me?" Here are a few of the responses I received:

- [ ] "I noticed that the boys in the back by my door never raise their hand and I never call on them. Then I noticed a group of girls at the front of the room always raises their hands. I switched the students, so the group of boys was in the front and the group of girls were in the back. I know the girls will continue to raise their hand, but this now puts the boys in front of me so I am more likely to call on them even if they don't raise their hand."
- [ ] "I feel like I move around my room when I lecture, but in the video, I noticed I move back and forth across the front of the room."

All of the teachers were assured that they did not have to share anything with me. In actuality I would say about twenty percent answered no when I asked if there were any ah-has they wanted to share. But those who did share had some great examples that affirmed the video lessons was a move in the right direction. Now we just needed a plan to take it to the next level.

As the videoing was winding down the first year, Melanie Stitt, a principal from another district, texted me a picture of something called a Swivel. (Melanie's husband was a teacher at my campus and he had discussed the videoing of lessons with her.) We looked into it and bought one to try out. Basically, you put an iPad or phone into the Swivel and wear a lanyard around your neck. The Swivel follows the lanyard while recording. We knew instantly that this is what we needed to take our lesson videoing to the next level.

As we began year two of videoing lessons, we now had three Swivels. Our assessment coordinator was overjoyed that she would not have to video each teacher. Instead, we asked her to create a Swivel Schedule and a plan to show teachers how to use the Swivel. She decided to set the schedule up by department (See Figure 3.2).

☐ Week 1 & 2	☐ 7th ELA
☐ Week 3	☐ 8th ELA
☐ Week 4	☐ 7th Math
☐ Week 5	☐ 8th Math
☐ Week 6	☐ 7th Science
☐ Week 7	☐ 8th Science
☐ Week 8	☐ 7th Social Studies
☐ Week 9	☐ 8th Social Studies

Figure 3.2: Swivel Schedule

Heather Sims, our assessment administrator, sent out the following Swivel Procedures to the teachers:

- ☐ I (Sims) will distribute the Swivel to the department (during dept. meeting time) with directions and review how to use it for about 10 minutes.
- ☐ Use the Swivel and your own device to video one class period.
- ☐ Take the Swivel and ALL parts to another teacher in your department.
- ☐ At the end of your designated week, I will collect the Swivel and ALL parts.
- ☐ If for some reason a teacher is not able to use the swivel during their week, they will need to check it out from the library before Spring Break.

The teachers were given the same reflective questions as the year before to look at while they watched their video. A few weeks after a department had the Swivel, we would go into their department meeting time and ask them to share any ah-has they had from their video with the department.

The teachers liked this method better because they had more say into the day and period they recorded, but they felt if we had a few more Swivels, it would make the process smoother. Teachers said it was too hard to move it from one teacher to the next and get it set up during a passing period. Based on teacher feedback we bought two more Swivels for the campus.

As a leader you must gather feedback from staff and actually listen to it. Knowing this, we asked our department chairs in August of year three, "How would you like to utilize the Swivels this year?" The answer we received was to table it until we get through the start of the new year. I put it on the department chair agenda for a September meeting and at that meeting it was suggested we table it until October. If you are in education, you know what October is like for teachers' state of mind. So, at a December meeting we brought it up again. The department chairs were not overly enthusiastic

School Transformation Through Teacher Appreciation

about getting a plan rolling, but they felt it was important. They suggested that they bring up at their planning sessions that the Swivels are in the library available for teachers to check out.

A handful of teachers recorded lessons they wanted to watch later and work on tweaking or enhancing. A few teachers recorded the students wanting to see "what" the students were doing while they were up at the front instructing. But overall, the Swivels were only checked out a few times.

As we began to wind down the year and start to look to the next year, I again put Swivel on the agenda. One of the department chairs said, "I really hoped that teachers would use the Swivel without a set plan in place. But, since they did not, can we create a plan that will allow us to continue in our transformation process without stringent timelines on it?" With this in mind we created a bit more of a structured plan moving into year four.

Each teacher was able to choose which lesson they wanted to record, check out a Swivel from the library, and record the lesson. The difference is this time they will watch the recorded lesson as a department. It can be a lesson they love and rock if that is what they are comfortable with, or it can be a lesson over something they struggle with and they want feedback and suggestions on. The only caveat is that they are done by spring break. During these conversations we would share that next year the plan will be for them to video something they struggle with and then watch it as a department so the other teachers can give them constructive feedback. In my experience if you tell teachers well in advance what is coming, they are not as shocked or upset when it gets here.

I got excited when a few teachers started videoing lessons on their own, not just the one I required. One teacher would video a class and ask the content coordinator for the district and myself to watch the video with her to give her input.

Entering year five I used conversations I had with the department chairs to steer us in the right direction. During August PD when departments were looking at their data from the previous year each teacher would establish which standard they struggled with the year before. That would be the standard the teacher would video a lesson from. When it was time for the teacher to teach that standard the teacher checked out a Swivel from the library and recorded their lesson teaching the designated standard. After recording the lesson, the department watched it together and gave the teacher constructive feedback on how the teacher can improve the lesson. Since the teachers will be recording a set standard and they appear at set times, the department chairs asked that there be no completion date. A few said the standards their department struggles with are after Spring Break.

When we started our journey, I did have some teachers who were uncomfortable when we started videoing because this was way outside of their comfort zone. When you try this, you have to take baby steps. If year one I had the teachers record a lesson based on their lowest standard and watch it as a department they would have revolted and rioted. But slowly working them through phases they were able to adapt with each step. Now my veterans are used to the process, and they are not threatened by videoing their lowest standard. This is a huge help when we have new teachers join us. My veterans are able to immediately reassure them that this is truly meant as a growth opportunity for teachers.

Data Room

How many times a day do you hear the word "data"? When I first became an administrator the only data, I was familiar with was state testing data. Over the years that followed I quickly learned there are LOTS of types of data, but the best and most powerful data is data that truly helps drive instruction and push student success. With this in mind, combined with teachers being very visual, our data room was born.

We have two grade levels at our school, 7th and 8th. Figure 3.3 is a picture of our 7th grade wall. There are four academic teams per grade level.

Figure 3.3: Data Posters

The yellow sign has the team name and the names of the teachers on that team. On each wall we also have keys to help with utilizing the data posters.

The first year we used data posters, the Texas Standardized State Assessment focused on student growth. We decided to use that as the focus of our data room. This meant that we listed out every student by team who did not experience growth on the state assessment the year before. As we moved through the year, we realized this concept did not give us the bang for our buck. A lot of the students listed were advanced students and we felt some of our lower achieving students fell through the cracks.

The following year, we decided to focus on closing the achievement gaps of our sub pops. We listed out students who fell into our lower achieving

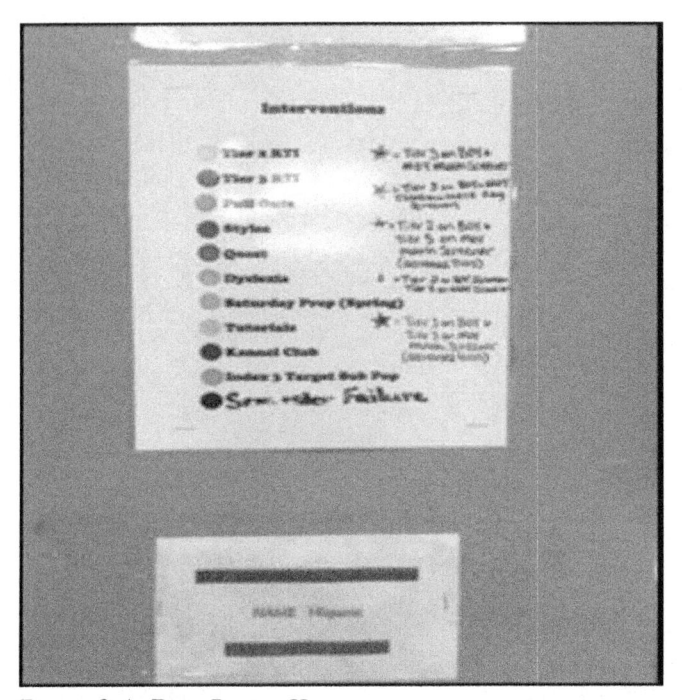

Figure 3.4: Data Poster Key

sub pops: special education, Hispanic, African American, economically disadvantaged, and at risk.

It was during this year that we started putting a key up beside each set of posters to explain what the various dots mean (see Figure 3.4).

As we moved into our third year, I knew we were on the right track when a teacher said, "I want to see all of my students." During this year we added a new part to the key where we highlighted which students were economically disadvantaged, Hispanic, and African American. These were our lowest performing sub pops, (See Figure 3.3 for key).

Our fourth year, I added a column to the data posters that said January Predictions. In this column the team was to write if they expected the student to pass each of their state assessments or not. If they wrote no, what was the plan to help that student?

As we started our fifth year with data posters, as part of our August professional development we grouped teachers by teams from the year before and had them look at their data posters, their state assessment results, and a reflective sheet. After they processed everything with their team, we then put them into their teams for the new school year and asked them "What do you want on your data posters for this year?" I loved all of the conversations I was hearing. During the debrief we were creating a list of what the teachers wanted when one teacher asked me if all of the teams needed to be the same. I thought, "Of course. I don't want to have to learn eight different data posters." My very next thought was these posters are not for me, they are for the teachers/teams. I told the teams they could put whatever they want on their poster, but I wanted to keep January Predictions on the posters. So, as we started the 2019-2020 school year, each team had data posters based on what they felt their needs were.

Technology Badging

My first three years on my new campus technology was one of our Campus Improvement Plan (CIP) goals. We would write goals such as *During the 2014-15 school year, teachers shall utilize technology in a minimum of two lessons per six weeks in order to incorporate 21st century learning into all classes.* Teachers would comply by doing two lessons each six weeks with technology incorporated.

I began to wonder, how can I make something I want the teachers to do engaging, fun, and competitive? With this thought in mind, I met with two of my teachers and my librarian. I knew I wanted to do "badging", but I had no idea how that would look. Thanks to the brilliance of Melanie Beatty, Ellen Crawford, and Kerri Harris, Hillwood Tech Badging was born.

When we started planning, we decided to create a competition by teacher and by department. When a teacher used a technology app or program, they simply filled out a quick reflection form. The tech badging team would pull up the reflection forms each week to see who has submitted for a badge and award the badges.

For the actual badges I bought a puzzle piece die cut. The tech badging team cut out puzzle pieces in various colors, printed a picture of the technology app or program, glued it to a puzzle piece, and put the badge in the teacher's box. Teachers then hung them outside of their classroom so others could see what badges they have earned, (see Figure 3.5). To incentivize the teachers, for each reflection they submitted their name was put into a drawing. Each month the tech badging team would draw five to ten names and give away jean passes, Super Sonic Drinks (see Chapter 9: Super Sonic Wednesday), and various other things.

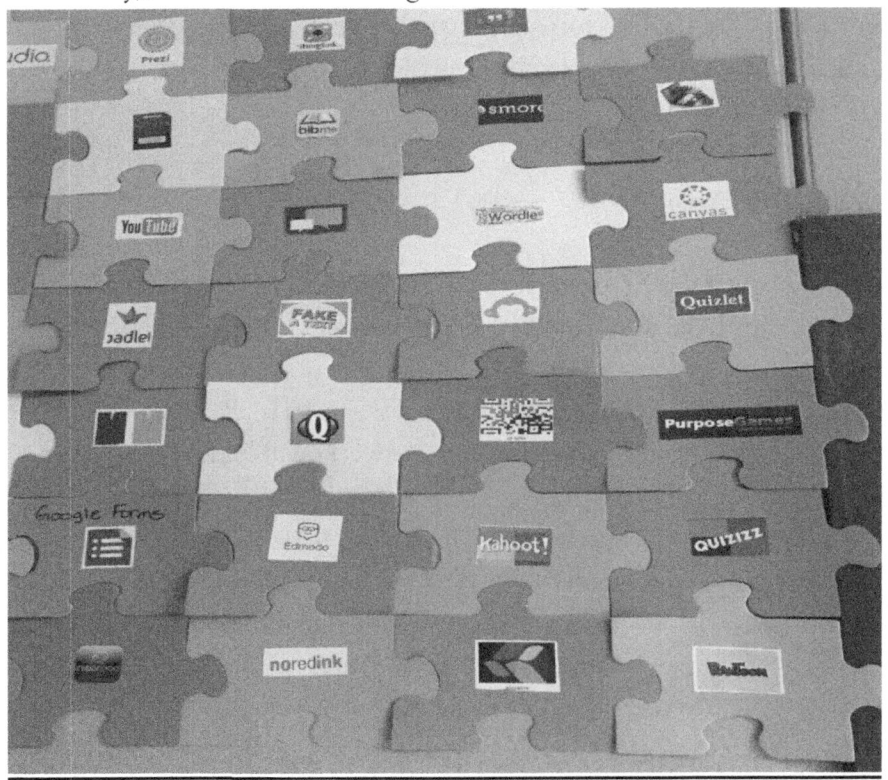

Figure 3.5: Tech Badges

School Transformation Through Teacher Appreciation

Technology Badging Information

Department Prizes

<u>End of Semester Winners</u> - Admin Team will cater a lunch for your department!

<u>End of Year Winners</u> - Mrs. Eckert will purchase a mini iPad cart specifically for the use of your department!

Individual Prizes

<u>Monthly Drawings</u> - For every puzzle piece you earn, your name will be entered into a drawing for various small prizes (i.e. jeans pass, Sonic drinks, small gift cards, etc.)!

<u>End of Year Winners</u> - Visa gift cards will be awarded for the top three winners: $100, $75, and $50! This is money to be used for your personal use - it doesn't have to be for your classroom.

Resource List

The list provided at this QR code can also be found on the posters in the lounge. Use this link as a quick reference when needed.

Badges?
Yes, we need our stinking badges!
Here's how it works!

1. Once you have finished the technology lesson with your students, it is required that you fill out the reflection piece found at this link: www.tinyurl.com/techbadge.

2. Once a week, the Tech Badge Committee will go through the reflections and distribute the badges to the appropriate places. The badges look like puzzle pieces.

3. Each individual will receive their badge to be placed above your classroom doorway.

4. After every member of the department has earned their individual badge for a specific technology, a department badge will be added to the wall in the lounge.

Figure 3.6: Technology Badging Plan

In the teacher's lounge the tech badging team created an area for each department. Once all of the teachers in a department earned a badge for a technology app or program the department would earn a badge that was put up in the teacher's lounge. This was huge in getting some of my non-techy teachers to try new things. The power of peer pressure. The department in the lead after the first semester got a lunch catered by the administration team and the end of year winning department got an iPad mini cart to keep in their department. The tech badging team created figure 3.6 to use when kicking off the program with the staff.

If you truly believe in something you have to give them the time and freedom to create. With this in mind I gave these ladies an extra conference and made it a common conference time. This allowed them to meet, collaborate, create staff presentations, and run the tech badging program they created. In addition to the common conference period, each year I sent the ladies to a technology conference to help them learn about new technology and learn how to use/incorporate the new technology.

The final layer we added in for year one was our campus librarian, Kerri Harris, did monthly professional development during our professional development period to show teachers new tools and items she had found and how they could use them in their classroom.

I am a firm believer in gathering input from your teachers, so we included a few questions about tech badging on the teacher end of year survey. The tech badging committee took that input and revamped tech badging.

The main piece of feedback we got from teachers was they wanted a way to see what teachers have used certain technology apps or programs so they can ask them specifics about it. We decided to use the open wall in our data room and post various technology apps and programs then list teacher's names under the technology they used. (See Figure 3.7 & 3.8)

We had a few other changes we made. First, as part of our new tech badging wall we created and posted a leaderboard in the room with the monthly leading department and teacher. (See Figure 3.9)

Figure 3.7: Technology Badging Wall

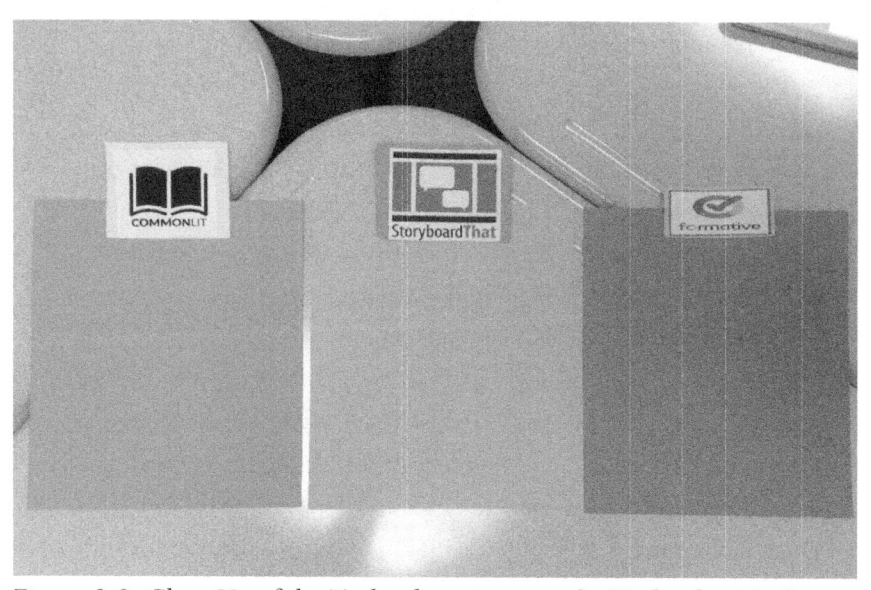

Figure 3.8: Close Up of the Technology Apps on the Technology Badging Wall

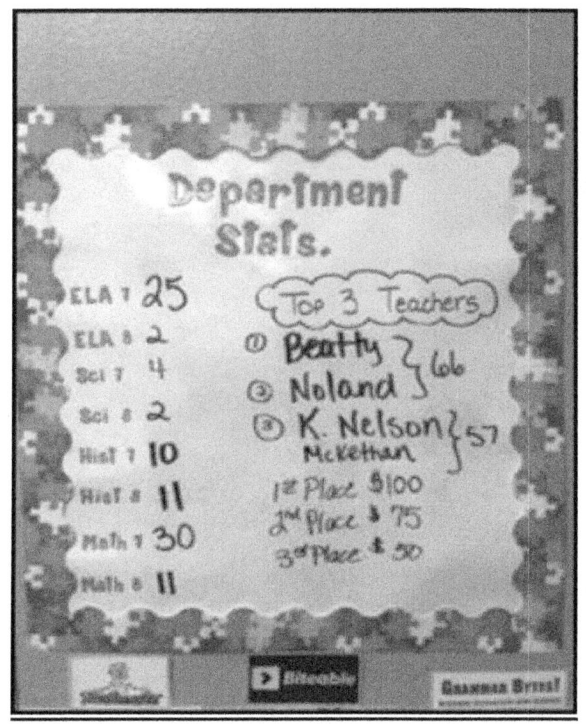

Figure 3.9: Technology Badging Leaderboard

    During this time, we were using the VESTED lesson plan model. We added to the Badge Reflection form a question that asked which part of the VESTED lesson plan model the piece of technology could be used with and that information was added to the sheet for that technology on the wall.

    The first year of tech badging the teacher was to "use" the technology. For year two the student was to "use" the technology.

    In year two we also added the Techie Teacher of the Month Award. The top badge earner for the month received the award. Dan Nelson, one of our math teachers, made a Techie Teacher of the Month plaque that the teacher could proudly display outside of their classroom. (See Figure 3.10) In addition to the monthly teacher recognition the lead department for that month got a one-hour lunch instead of the normal 30 minutes. Once a month

Figure 3.10: Techie Teacher of the Month Award

we have hour lunches for students by grade level. Teachers get a 30 minute lunch and they supervise the 30 minutes opposite of their lunch. The department that submitted the most tech badges that month got the full hour for lunch and no duty.

When it was time to wrap up year two, we once again reached out to the teachers to get their input. On the teacher end of year survey, we asked two questions about tech badging: how can tech badging be taken to the next level and what suggestions do you have for teacher and department incentives for technology badging?

As we began year three, the tech badging team decided to utilize Canvas (the district preferred classroom platform). The team created a menu of badges from which the teachers could "shop". Teachers scrolled through the badges and clicked on "Badge Quick View" links to see a quick rundown of what the digital tool could do. If they want to learn more, they click on another link in the module. There was a video tutorial for every badge. In addition to this, the teachers submitted their badges through Canvas as well.

With the move to Canvas, the initial training was revamped as well. The training was adjusted to run more like a giant PBL project. Teachers worked on DIY's (researching the Canvas site for new badges) and the badging team ran workshops at the same time for specific technology tools. Teachers could request a workshop by emailing the new HMS-Badging email address. Our librarian, Kerri Harris, also decided to change up her monthly PD. Departments were given three options:

- ☐ If you want to use the time for your DIY's of submitting badges, then that time can be used for that purpose.
- ☐ If you would like to use that time to get information from the tech badging team on different kinds of technology for your classes, then your time can be used for that. You'll just need to let the tech badging team know what you need from them in that regard so they can do the research ahead of time.
- ☐ If you would like to come in and just learn about new technology and are open to hear about anything that might work, then the tech badging team will make sure they are prepared with several ideas that will apply to all subjects.

In addition to the monthly PD Kerri started Tech Tuesday with a Twist where she would blog each Tuesday about technology and email the link to the staff.

The purpose of starting technology badging was to get our teachers to use technology in their classrooms as an instructional tool. The tech badging team met towards the end of the third year and came to the conclusion that teachers were using technology to enhance student learning. Based on this the team decided technology badging had done what it was intended to do. We would in essence "take this off of their plate". Our librarian continued to still conduct monthly professional development sessions during the PD period about technology tools to ensure the teachers were seeing and learning about new pieces of technology they could incorporate into their classes.

When we took this "off their plate" we did make sure they knew we were doing so and why. It can be very powerful for staff to know you are taking something "off their plate". But be cautious of them thinking it was a fade or an initiative they simply needed to just outwait. For us technology badging transformed from an initiative to being the norm at our school.

We never "required" teachers to participate in or submit tech badges! Through competition and recognition most of our teachers wanted to participate and those who did not periodically got pressure from their department to submit badges so the department could get credit for certain technology tools. Technology badging can always be brought back for a year and made a fun competition if we see the need.

Give Them Voice

In August 2018, teachers were split by department, and each was given chart paper and markers. I asked them to create a T chart. On the left I asked them to list instructional initiatives and on the right list school climate initiatives. As the teachers collaborated and created their charts, I asked them to put a D by any of the initiatives that were district initiatives. Once they were done, I asked them, "What can we take off of your plates and how."

I started by giving them an example. At this point we had been doing technology badging for four years. We began badging because we needed our teachers to look at and experiment with a variety of technology tools to help engage the students and increase student achievement. I realized during the fourth year of badging that it had become natural for our teachers to look for and try new technology tools. Since it was now a normal practice for us there was no need to continue the technology badging initiative, so we have taken that off their plates.

The input from the groups was compiled and added to our bi-weekly department chair meetings. This list became part of our meetings until as a team we had worked our way through the list and made changes that were collaborated and decided on by the department chairs. As decisions were made the department chairs shared them with their departments.

This was a great exercise for us, but please keep in mind I did this at the beginning of my seventh year at the campus. If you use this strategy, you MUST be ready for blunt input and work to not let your defensiveness show. (We all get defensive when our baby is criticized. It is human nature.)

Chapter Four
Utilize Your Community & School Organizations

Donations

    Businesses around your school are more than willing to donate to your campus if asked. My favorite times to contact our local businesses are when I am gearing up for August professional development and teacher appreciation week. When I contact them, I ask for gift cards, items, and/or coupons. For August PD I use items as door prizes and for Twitter Challenges. For teacher appreciation week I use items for random drawings for teachers.

Scavenger Hunt

    When I first came to Hillwood it was about three weeks before the teachers started back, and I had ZERO money for our back-to-school PD week. Situations like this are the best time to get creative! I decided to send the teachers into our neighborhood on a scavenger hunt and I wanted to include community businesses. I contacted twenty businesses and asked them if they would participate. The plan was to place a QR code inside the business door, the team would scan the QR code, learn about something from the faculty handbook, and then need to "get" a certain item from that location to bring back to the school. Some examples are:

- ☐ Home Depot: get a paint stirrer.
- ☐ Racetrac gas station: get a free fountain drink.
- ☐ Subway: get a free cookie.

    On the day of the scavenger hunt as the teachers came into the library, I gave them a playing card. (At this point they had no idea what was about to happen.) The plan was for 20 groups of 4 staff members each. Once everyone was seated, I explained we were about to go on a scavenger hunt. Remember, I said I had zero money, so I told them that the first group back with all of the items would get a class covered day where an administrator would take their classes for a day while they plan or work on anything they wanted to work on.

Teachers were told to find their group members by partnering with the teachers who had the same playing card they had. Once they had their group, they were to come get a QR code from me and go. I had 20 different QR codes. This allowed me to have the groups start at different locations to help prevent bottlenecking.

It warmed my heart when some of the businesses started calling me and thanking me for asking them to participate. The restaurants said some of the groups would move the QR code, but when the next group came in looking the customers were telling them where the other group moved it to. Other community members share fun stories as well.

For this next part, if you decide to try it, make sure your staff has a good sense of humor. I worked with my secretary and one of my assistant principals to identify four teachers I could have some fun with. For those four I put their cards on the bottom of the playing cards I was handing out as teachers came in to ensure those four were grouped up. When we cut the groups lose my secretary and assistant principal were each waiting in a staff parking lot to see what car the group got in and they took a picture of the license plate.

Once all of the groups were back in the library, we started debriefing the activity. While we were talking Mike Stitt, one of the coaches, said, "Oh s***, the cops are here." I turned and looked at Coach Stitt and said, "huh"? Coach Stitt then said, "He has a ticket book." I walked to the library door and stepped just outside of the door. The officer asked for Mary Anderson, the owner of the vehicle the group had gotten in for the scavenger hunt. Danny Montemayor jumped up with her and said he was driving. The officer was talking to them outside of the library and asked for the rest of their group to come out into the hall. Magen Rabatin and Tre John joined the other two.

School Transformation Through Teacher Appreciation

Pause for a moment, the teachers were so shocked and focused on the officer that they didn't see me step back into the library, grin because I just couldn't help it, and signal to Shawnda Neyland, one of the coaches I had videoing the encounter, to come into the hall.

Back to the story. The officer told the group that when they pulled out of the Dollar Tree parking lot, they caused a wreck behind them. One of the cars involved in the wreck was a black Lincoln that had a visiting state senator in it. The officer continued to talk about the accident and their responsibility for about three minutes. At that point I put my hand out to shake his hand and said, "What was your name again?" He replied, "Chief Deputy Eckert" as he took my hand. I said, "Hi sweetheart" and kissed him on the cheek.

Immediately you heard teachers in the library say, "She kissed him." It took the teachers from the group a few seconds to catch on. When they did, one sat down on the floor. After I walked my husband into the library and told the staff, "I wanted you all to meet my husband since you will be seeing him up here a lot."

My secretary told me the next day that the staff blew up Facebook saying it was the best professional development day that had ever had, and they were looking forward to working with their new principal. A few weeks after that, the new superintendent came to walk the campus during the school day and that was my first time to meet him, as I was hired by an interim superintendent. When I introduced myself to him, he said, "You are the principal who pranked her staff." I nervously smiled at him, and he said his secretary told him all about it and he loved it. Turns out Danny Montemayor's mom was the superintendent's secretary, but my co-conspirators left that part out.

Again, use caution if you try to do the officer part. But a scavenger hunt is a great way to get your staff out in your community and help them see where your students live.

Step Contest

Our state has our teachers watch active monitoring videos each year and as a district/campus, we REALLY push teachers to be up and moving around as they actively monitor. One day at a safety fair hosted by the Sheriff's Department, we saw an insurance company handing out pedometers when inspiration struck. We decided to create a step contest for state testing. I contacted a Farmers Insurance representative that I have partnered with in the past to see if she would buy me a set of step counters with her logo on them. She agreed, so I then crafted a plan.

Teachers who wanted to participate checked out a step counter each morning by a certain time. They would wear the counter while they "actively monitored" the students who were testing. At the end of the day the teachers would turn in their step counter. I had an office lady who logged teacher steps daily. Prizes were given each day to the teacher with the most steps and then there was one grand prize for the teacher with the most steps overall after all of our testing days were completed. Our teachers loved how we were able to add some competitive fun to their required active monitoring.

Restaurants

Contact restaurants in your area to see if they would like to partner with you to help you recognize your teachers. Things like this can be a win-win for both of you. The restaurant gets a tax write off and advertising while the teachers get something extra to make them feel special. A few partnerships I have done are:
- ☐ Chili's gave us a Chili's gift set for our teacher of the month awards. The set included a few Chili's promotional items and a $10 gift card.
- ☐ Fresco's (Mexican Restaurant) gave us a $25 gift certificate for our House Point Wizard of the month. (See Chapter 3: Houses)

Insurance Companies

School Transformation Through Teacher Appreciation

For the Step Contest I shared how Farmers Insurance purchased pedometers for a contest during our state assessment, (see Chapter 4: Step Contest). Another way Farmers Insurance has partnered with us is with monthly drawings. Farmers put a box in our workroom. Teachers simply wrote their name on a slip of paper and dropped it in the box. The Farmers agent would come to the school, draw a name, and empty the box. Then she would email the teacher and ask her to email a list of items they wanted from Amazon up to $100. The Farmers agent would buy the items, arrange them in a cute arrangement, and bring them to the school to present to the teacher. After the presentation, Farmers would post pictures of the teachers with her items on their social media accounts, and I would post them on our school social media accounts and tag the agent in the posts. As with the restaurants, this is a win-win for both of us.

Another insurance company we partner with is Horace Mann. An agent came to meet with me to discuss ways we could partner. We came up with a few ways for them to help us with some fun student incentives, but I also wanted something for teachers. The agent shared with me that Horace Mann could give us two crystal apple awards a year that we would give to teachers. I ran with the idea, and we created the Above and Beyond Award, (see Chapter 7: Above and Beyond Award). I like to give out both awards at the January or February pep rally. The administrators collaborate and pick the two teachers based on whatever we want to give it for. The agent comes to the pep rally to help present the awards and I tell the students and staff why the teacher is receiving our Above and Beyond Award. I try to look for those teachers I tend to gravitate towards when I need special things. A few examples:

- ☐ Kerri Harris, our librarian, has received one. Kerri is always asking to help create lessons with teachers and help them teach it, coming up with creative ways to get students to read, conducting PDs for our staff, and many more things.

☐ Todd Nevitt, our audio/visual teacher, has received one. Todd is my go-to person when I need videos made, from teacher of the year videos to PSA videos I need created for students.

Investment/Retirement Companies

Most schools get calls from investment groups wanting to speak to their staff about retirement plans, etc. One particular group talks to our teachers during lunch faculty meetings each year, (see Chapter 1: Faculty Meetings). I wanted to do something fun with my staff when they return in August, but money was tight. So, I contacted the group and asked if they wanted to set up a table at our Preview Nights where parents and students pick up their schedules and such in August. I have never had a business set up, so I thought it would be a prime night for the investment group. In return I asked them to pick up the tab for my staff to go bowling for two hours, and the following year I asked them to pay for that staff to go to a trampoline park. (See Chapter 6: Make It Fun).

Real Estate Agents

One of the best partnerships I have is with a local real estate agent. Amanda Steelman used to teach for me and when she had her son, Luke she went into business with her mom and sister so she could spend more time with her son. The Spurrier group shows love for our teachers in many ways. From providing lunch at a faculty meeting to helping with We Love October and We Love February, (see Chapter 6: Make It Fun) to putting simple things in teacher boxes, (see Figure 4.1).

Amanda has easily helped twenty of our staff members buy houses in the past few years. The staff that has bought and sold homes with her is not just staff who worked at Hillwood when she taught there, but also staff new to our campus. This partnership is simply amazing!

Figure 4.1: Flyer and Treat Put into Teacher Boxes

You are probably thinking Amanda does so much with us because she used to work with us. Honestly, that is how it started, but now she does things for us because of the amount of business she gets from our staff. Today's younger teachers don't stay in a house for ten plus years. They buy and sell their homes with a lot more frequency. If you were going to develop a partnership with just one community member, make it an awesome realtor.

Student Organizations

When planning We Love October, We Love February, (see Chapter 6: Make It Fun), and Teacher Appreciation Week, (see Chapter 8: Value Them as a Person), I like to incorporate NJHS, AVID, STUCO, PALS, Choir, etc. The first time I reached out to student organizations was when I was planning Teacher Appreciation Week. I asked a few of them if they wanted to provide breakfast or snacks for the staff one day during the week. I was blown away at how much the students and sponsors enjoyed doing something for the staff. Like I said earlier in the book about parents, sometimes they just need to know more specific ways they can help.

Figure 4.2: National Bubble Gum Day from AVID

    The second year we did We Love October and We Love February. I looked at a national day's calendar and created a list of national days during those months. Then, when asking student organizations for ideas, I included those days. I assured them that I would love anything they wanted to do, but I discovered sometimes they need ideas. Here are a few examples:
- National Chocolate Mint Day - NJHS
- National Bubble Gum Day - AVID (see Figure 4.2)
- National Tortilla Chip Day - School Pride & Spirit
- National Eat Fruit at Workday - STUCO

Part II:
Momentum

Chapter Five
Support Your Teachers

Individual Teacher Meetings

Some of the best things come about when you least expect it. This strategy was derived when I knew I would be having foot surgery during Thanksgiving break, and I knew I would need to be off of my feet as much as possible between the Thanksgiving and Christmas breaks. I wanted to make sure I did not lose touch with my teachers during those weeks, so I set up individual teacher meetings in thirty-minute increments.

This happened to be the first year we had teachers video a lesson, so I decided to roll that into these meetings, (see Chapter 3: Teacher Video Reflections). I created a set of questions that I asked and took notes on during each meeting.

- ☐ What is one thing you would not change about the school?
- ☐ What is one thing you would change?
- ☐ What is something you have never tried, but you are considering?
- ☐ Where do you see yourself in 5 years?
- ☐ What can I do to support you?
- ☐ Any "Ah-ha" moments in your video?

After the meetings I typed up the responses to the 2nd question and put what the plan was to address each requested change.

I really enjoyed these meetings and so did the teachers, so I decided to do them again the following year with different questions.

- ☐ What is something you have tried in your classroom for the first time? How did it go?
- ☐ What has caused you the most stress this year?
- ☐ What do you hope your students will remember most about you as a teacher?
- ☐ What do you need more staff development in?

School Transformation Through Teacher Appreciation

☐ What can I do to support you?

As I began to look towards the third year of conducting individual meetings, I decided to revamp them a tad. All teachers who were new to the school I scheduled a fall and spring "Check-In" meeting with them. During the first meeting I asked them a combination of the questions from the first two years depending on the teacher and how our conversation was going. For returning teachers I put out an email in the fall and an email in the spring simply saying if you would like a thirty-minute meeting with me for any reason, please let me know. Most of my teachers simply call, text, email, or come see me if they need me, but the reserved ones feel more comfortable asking for a meeting when I send out the email. At these meetings, I have no questions. I let the teacher know this is their meeting and they have my undivided attention for thirty minutes.

Tip: Turn over your cell phone, turn off your office phone ringer, and close your door during these meetings. The teacher you are meeting with deserves your undivided attention.

Professional Development Books

Let's face it: we are faced with many constraints when it comes to purchasing things for our teachers. If your teachers are true lifelong learners they purchase books for professional development purposes. A great way to support your teachers is to combine these two. If the books are to improve instruction, you should be able to use campus funds to purchase the books.

Most of my teachers know I will purchase books for them if they simply ask, but I still like to mention this a few times a year at faculty meetings.

Partner with Other Schools

It has become very apparent that teachers cannot operate in silos, and the same goes for schools. Partner with the other schools in your district that have the same grade levels and if your school is the only one in your district reach out to schools in surrounding districts. There is a LOT of power in sharing and collaborating with other schools. I am fortunate to have six other middle schools in my district.

Debbie Silver is an amazing and funny speaker. I had the privilege of seeing her at a conference and thought it would be great to have her talk to my staff in January when the teachers return from their holiday break, and we are gearing up for the second half of the school year. I contacted the other middle schools in my district, divided the cost up among the campuses, and used a high school's auditorium.

Jack Breckemeyer has a great book called *Taming the Team*. I saw him do a keynote about the book and immediately decided I wanted him to work with my teams. For this endeavor I partnered with two other middle schools in my district. We designed the day, so Jack worked with the team leaders from all three campuses in the morning and all of the teams in the afternoon to begin building their plans.

Now Jack is also very funny! A few years later we brought Jack back out to work with the middle school teachers for all of the middle schools in our district. Jack presented his PD, *Teaching Strategies to Motivate Middle School Students*. We did this in January when the teachers were getting ready to start the second half of the year. Jack did a great job of making the teachers laugh, energizing them for the new semester, and demonstrated strategies I later saw several of my teachers using in their classes.

Another great way to partner with schools is to simply share ideas. When I first came to the district, they didn't have PD or collaboration sessions where teachers from various schools were together. I reached out to the other middle school principals and created a plan for use to share data and collaborate, (see Figure 5.1 & 5.2).

School Transformation Through Teacher Appreciation

KISD Middle School Planning Day

Today's Objective: To build collaboration amongst campuses to increase student achievement on specific SEs.

- Each teacher needs to have access to their lesson plans for 2012-2013 and the scope and sequence for their content area.
- The facilitator will give each teacher:
  - *Heat Maps* for their grade level content from all 5 middle schools.
  - Blank *Teacher Perception Data Collection Tool* form (by grade level content).

Facilitators:

- Have the teachers use the 5 campus heat maps to fill out the *Teacher Perception Data Collection Tool* form. (This should only take about 10 minutes)
  - As a group, select 2 district focus areas all 5 campuses need to work on.
  - Select 1 campus focus, in addition to the 2 district focuses each campus will work on.
  - (Facilitator – list the district (2) and each campus' (1) focus SE on the form provided. You will leave this form with Mrs. Eckert and she will scan and email them to Mrs. Anderson.)
  - Of the 3 SEs identified by the group, which ones are taught before Jan. 24? (All 5 campuses will be meeting again Jan. 24. On that day they can discuss the SEs taught after Jan. 24.) (Fill this info in on the chart from above.)
- Look at the 2 district SEs that the group identified.
  - How did each campus teach this SE?
  - What part do they feel their students struggled with?
  - What can be done to address the issues discussed?
  - Looking back, what would they tweak or change?
  - Where there any pitfalls to watch for?
  - How can VESTED be used to teach the SE?
- Look at the 1 campus SE identified.
  - How did each campus teach this SE?
  - What part do they feel their students struggled with?
  - What can be done to address the issues discussed?
  - Looking back, what would they tweak or change?
  - Where there any pitfalls to watch for?
  - How can VESTED be used to teach the SE?

Figure 5.1: KISD Middle School Planning Day Plan

Department _____ Grade Level _____

		When does it occur		When does it occur
KISD Goals				
FHMS Goal				
ISMS Goal				
HMS Goal				
KMS Goal				
TSMS Goal				

Facilitator: After your session is complete – reflect on the discussion that took place in your room. List below a few names of teachers you think might be good candidates to write lessons for the district based on what you observed today. **Please do not share this information with the teachers.** This is still in the developmental stages.

Please return this form to the from office at Hillwood.

Thank you for your assistance today!!!

Figure 5.2: KISD Middle School Planning Day Data Sheet

KISD Middle School Planning Day

Today's Objective: To build collaboration amongst campuses to increase student achievement on specific SEs.

- Each teacher needs to have access to their lesson plans for last year, the scope and sequence for their content area, and assessment data from when the chosen SEs were taught.

Facilitators:

Each facilitator will have a copy of the Oct. 4 SEs for each teacher, a plus/delta sheet, and a PDSA sheet.

Have teachers sit in groups with one teacher from each campus in each group. If a campus has more teachers than other campuses then they can double up in a group. The key is to have all 5 campuses represented in each group.

Please stop any negativity during the discussions. If a teacher goes off on a tangent please redirect them.

- Give each teacher a copy of the Oct. 4 SEs.
- Look at the SEs listed for KISD and each individual campus.
  - Which SEs have already been taught this year?
    - Lead your group thru a plus/delta for each SE that has already been taught this year. (One at time)
  - Which SEs have not been taught yet?
    - Facilitator will lead group through deconstruction of one of those SEs followed by lesson development:

      Process to follow:
      - Identify **nouns** and **noun phrases** to identify key concepts.
      - Locate **verbs** to identify key target(s).
      - Place the targets into one or more **Learning Target categories**.
      - Identify the **learning progression**.
      - Clarify terms that may lead to multiple interpretations.
      - Construct a list of skills that are essential to become proficient in the identified standard.
    - Lead your group thru a PDSA for each SE that has not been taught yet this year.
      - Consider:
        - Look at the plus/delta from the SEs already taught. How can you use this information when deciding "how" to teach these SEs?

When you finish doing this will all of the SEs allow the teachers to have the remaining time for collaboration.

Figure 5.3: KISD Middle School Planning Follow Up Day

The initial joint planning day was done in October. All of the principals got such good feedback from their teachers that we decided to do a follow up day in January. At the second session the teachers used the information from the October meetings and expanded upon what they had done, (see Figure 5.3)

Chapter Six
Make it fun

Bowling (Community Member Paid)

Assign teams and take your staff to the local bowling alley for a fun afternoon of team-building and friendly competition. Have teachers keep track of points and give prizes for highest score and lowest score for both individuals and teams. We did this in August as a back-to-school team builder at the end of our first day when the teachers returned. I made a fun award presentation that we used to kick off our PD sessions the next day.

Altitude Trampoline Park (Community Member Paid)

After doing home visits to 535 7th grade houses, we went and played at the trampoline park for two hours. Everyone wants to be a kid again! Bring teachers to the trampoline park and let them jump for joy at the beginning of a new school year. Our male staff had a flip contest, others played dodgeball and climbed a rock wall, and some just sat, socialized, and laughed at those playing. It was a great time of fellowship.

Community Scavenger Hunt

Prior to the in-service day, hit up local businesses and restaurants to garner support for your school through coupons, gift certificates, and free trinkets. When teachers enter the school building, use a deck of playing cards to divide your teachers into teams and send them on a wild goose chase through the local community. Each team will get in a car, drive to a different location, and then follow the clues by scanning QR codes at local businesses and restaurants. The first team that completes the scavenger hunt and makes it back to school without getting a ticket or having a wreck wins a prize! If anyone on your staff is competitive, this will be one of their most memorable training days ever. It also helps gain involvement from community partners and stakeholders who can be a valuable asset to your school for years to come, (Chapter 4: Utilize Your Community & Student Organizations).

Goosechase

Goosechase brings scavenger hunts into the digital world, and they are a lot of fun. You are able to set up different types of tasks/activities and assign how many points you want each activity to be worth. For the tasks/activities as you create them you designate if the participants need to upload a picture, answer a question, or be at a certain GPS location. The first time we did a staff Goosechase during a professional development day I designed it as a "learn our community" game. For instance, upload a picture of someone from your team taking shopping carts from the parking lot into the store or driving through an apartment complex where students live. This can be used as a fun game, but also allow your staff to see where your students live.

A few years ago, our district moved to a feeder pattern system for our schools. To help build team unity between our campuses from elementary to high school, I created a Goosechase. (When using Goosechase you can assign teams or have the participants pick teams.) For this one, I chose to assign teams that were composed of two elementary school teachers, one middle school teacher, and one high school teacher. Each team was assigned a shape and color. For instance, orange circle or purple triangle. All schools met in the high school auditorium. Hillwood teachers were given a sign to hold up for their assigned group so the elementary and high school teachers could easily meet up with their assigned group.

Then I decided to also incorporate various community members who I partner with during the school year. My thought was I would expose the community members to a larger audience base, and it would be a way of thanking that community member. For instance, we have a close partnership with The Spurrier Group Realtors, so one of the tasks was to go to a location where they were set up and take a business card.

School Transformation Through Teacher Appreciation

Some tasks incorporated various people from our school district and school locations. One of the most popular tasks was to take a selfie with your whole team and the superintendent. I had told him to hide and put out random tweet clues about his location. This task was worth the most points possible. He hid for a while, but eventually most of the teams located him.

As part of this Goosechase, we gave them a Twitter Challenge, (See Chapter 6: Twitter Challenge). Our superintendent is a huge Twitter person, so at the end of the Goosechase I had him give out the prizes for the Twitter Challenge. Before he started to give out the prizes, he told the participants that they were trending number six in DFW with our hashtag. That means a lot of people got to see our staff bonding and having fun in our community.

Transformations

Transform your school's library or cafeteria to create a new environment for learning and team building. Here are 3 ways:

1. Create an operating room for teachers to deconstruct your state's learning standards. Start by having teachers don scrubs, lab coats, and surgeon masks donated by a parent or PTA member with connections to a medical facility. Let teachers take a pre-assessment of their knowledge that will send them either to triage, surgery, or recovery based on their score. Then have district facilitators or your school's administrators at each different "hospital wing" to help guide teachers through the deconstruction process at their previously determined pace. Bring the entire staff back together at the end of the day to debrief and address concerns and celebrations.
2. Tell your staff to dress casual and bring their sunglasses and lawn chairs to professional development days for beach-themed fun. Create a photo booth using a beach or Hawaiian face cut-out so teachers can take goofy pics and selfies with

their friends. Decorate tables with luau flowers, hula skirts, and cheap dollar store décor.
3. Circle around a "campfire" for professional development days. Decorate with tents, lawn chairs, and a fake campfire to help teachers feel relaxed and refreshed as they begin a new school year. Or, if your climate is mild enough, take your staff outside to a real campfire and conduct the days' activities there.

The best part of this is after we finished with the decorations, they were put into tubs the teachers could use to transform their classrooms.

Carnival

Everyone loves a carnival! Bring in former students or student leaders from an organization like National Honor Society to work the carnival booths while your teachers have fun. Create game booths using items from your school, donations from PTA/parents, or use some budget money to order inexpensive games from companies like Oriental Trading. Use cheap Home Depot tool belts for workers to keep supplies and tickets in, and let teachers travel through the carnival at their own pace and earn tickets. Utilize break times and team-building times throughout the week to give your staff a chance to visit all the carnival booths. At the end of the PD days, you can auction off a few big items and/or let participants use their tickets to buy prizes in a store full of goofy and fun items. Prizes can include toys (to give to students as incentives throughout the year), office supplies, candy, jean passes, coupons, etc. Everyone will leave with a smile on their face! One teacher later said, "I still remember the "nose/nostril" pencil sharpener I got that day—you had to stick the pencil up the nose to sharpen it—so perfect for middle school!!"

The year I did the carnival I had students in the gym with the games all day. I bought them lunch and they simply hung out, played games, and socialized between the times teachers were in the gym. Then, instead of adding team builders into the agenda, I combined the breaktime and the time I

School Transformation Through Teacher Appreciation

> **Come One, Come All**
> **Hillwood Middle School**
> **August Staff Development**
>
> **When:** Monday, August 19, thru
> Monday, August 26,
> **Time:** 8:00 am - 4:00 pm each day
> **Where:** Hillwood Middle School Cafeteria
> **Dress:** Jeans
>
> Come ready to learn and hopefully have a little fun as well!

Figure 6.1: Teacher Invitation

would have used for team building and gave them 30 minutes for *Break and Playtime*, (see Figure 6.2). This way teachers can decide to use the time how they want. It was hilarious watching the teachers trying to cheat at games and the students calling them out. Both the teachers who participated and the students had a blast on those days. The items from the staff carnival were placed into tubs and were made available for teachers to use in their classrooms.

Monday, August 19

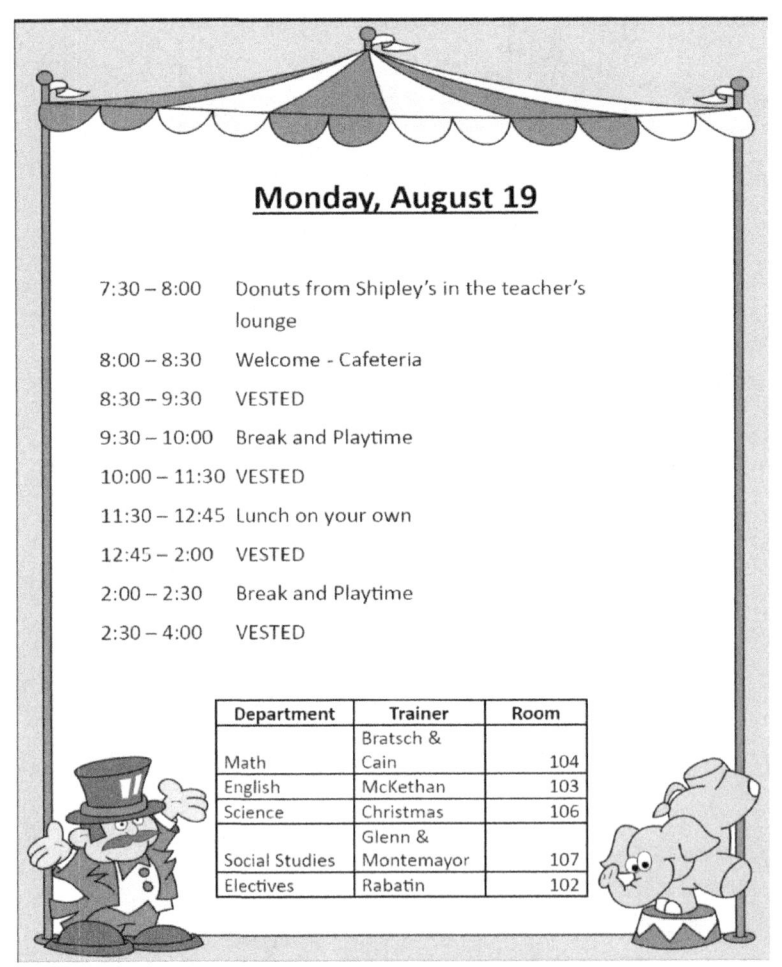

7:30 – 8:00	Donuts from Shipley's in the teacher's lounge
8:00 – 8:30	Welcome - Cafeteria
8:30 – 9:30	VESTED
9:30 – 10:00	Break and Playtime
10:00 – 11:30	VESTED
11:30 – 12:45	Lunch on your own
12:45 – 2:00	VESTED
2:00 – 2:30	Break and Playtime
2:30 – 4:00	VESTED

Department	Trainer	Room
Math	Bratsch & Cain	104
English	McKethan	103
Science	Christmas	106
Social Studies	Glenn & Montemayor	107
Electives	Rabatin	102

Figure 6.2: Professional Development Agenda

HMS Olympics

HMS Olympics was created by Craig Weston who was an assistant principal at the campus. The teachers were placed into groups in advance and then had to work their way through various stations. Stations included knocking things down with water guns, relays on the track, trivia, etc. The teams decide who from their team will participate in which event.

School Transformation Through Teacher Appreciation

A few years later when we were gearing up to start our house system with our feeder campus, we took the HMS Olympics to the next level. Bronwyn Sullenberger, one of our assistant principals, built on Craig's work. Bronwyn teamed our teachers with teachers from our feeder campus. For our joint Olympics she incorporated frisbee relay around the school, bowling down water bottles with a golf ball in a pantihose on their head, scooter races down the halls, etc.

A/B Honor Roll Celebration

A few years ago, Texas went to a letter grade accountability system for schools and districts. There were many flaws with the system and many superintendents were speaking out against the system. That being said, our school received all As and Bs. I am always telling my teachers to teach the state standards to master level and the state assessment results will come. So, when we had great scores, even in a flawed system, we had to celebrate.

I decorated our PD room with large A and B balloons, bought A/B Honor Roll buttons, and we had cupcakes with punch. As a campus we took time to celebrate our accomplishments and to give the teachers the recognition they deserved. Due to the issues with the system, I asked teachers to please not share with their friends from other campuses our celebration. Then I proceeded to show my teachers how the system is flawed. The point is we took time to celebrate when there was something to celebrate.

Fabulous February

In January 2019, I read a blog post from Amber Teamann called Fab Fridays in February about ideas to make February fun for your staff. Knowing I was limited by money constraints, I created Fabulous February, (see Figure 6.3). At the January faculty meeting each teacher received a colored copy of Fabulous February.

Fabulous February

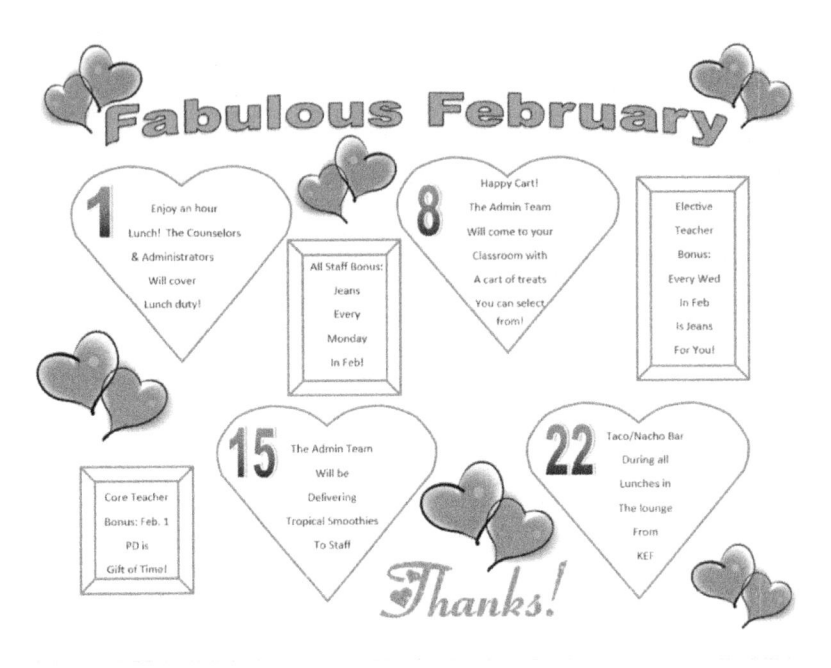

1 — Enjoy an hour Lunch! The Counselors & Administrators Will cover Lunch duty!

All Staff Bonus: Jeans Every Monday In Feb!

8 — Happy Cart! The Admin Team Will come to your Classroom with A cart of treats You can select from!

Elective Teacher Bonus: Every Wed In Feb Is Jeans For You!

Core Teacher Bonus: Feb. 1 PD is Gift of Time!

15 — The Admin Team Will be Delivering Tropical Smoothies To Staff

22 — Taco/Nacho Bar During all Lunches in The lounge From KEF

Thanks!

Figure 6.3: Fabulous February

We Love October & We Love February

My staff enjoyed Fabulous February so much that I decided to ratchet it up a few notches and create We Love October by doing something every day in October. I began with a blank calendar of October and filled in jeans days we already had scheduled as part of our Color Out Days, Payday Breakfast (see Chapter 9: Payday Breakfast), and the faculty meeting since lunch is always provided. Next, I looked to see what day hour lunches were scheduled for the students during October. I talked to my campus administrative team to see if everyone would be on campus that day so we could give the teachers an hour lunch that day as well. That conversation led to my counselors offering to do a Staff Care Day (see Chapter 8: Staff Care Day). From there I looked at the national day calendar to see if I could incorporate any national theme days. I found two that I thought we could use, National Chocolate Covered Pretzel Day and National Chocolate Day.

School Transformation Through Teacher Appreciation

Our PTA is amazing! They normally provide lunch for the staff three times during the year: back to school, Christmas, and Teacher Appreciation Week. I contacted my PTA president and asked if we could move the back-to-school lunch to October and I shared with her what I was planning. She loved it, so I asked if we could move the Christmas lunch to February since the wheels in my head were already spinning for February.

At this point we only had a few days left to fill in. One of my assistant principals, Bronwyn Sullenberger, asked to take a day for her club School Pride & Spirit to do something. I immediately said of course and asked her if she wanted to plan some fun games for our staff to play on the campus professional development day scheduled for October 11. Bronwyn created forty-five minutes of magic and laughter. Staff played truth or dare Jenga, had magic carpet races, and picked up marbles with their feet.

Most of the days were filled in except for Wednesdays. I talked to my administration team and asked if they would be willing to make cookies for the teachers for a cookie day. I plugged two teacher treats in, (see Chapter 7: Teacher Treats), and decided on smoothies for the last two Wednesdays.

Don't Sweat It

Find the Pumpkin

Popcorn Delivery

Room Service (See Chapter 9: Room Service)

In the November faculty meeting, I collected input from the teachers using two questions: What was your favorite part about We Love October and what suggestions do you have for We Love February?
Here are a few things the staff said they liked about We Love October:

- ☐ *I absolutely loved having something to look forward to each day that month! Sometimes it is the little things that can improve one's day. I genuinely felt appreciated that month. Sweats days were my favorite because I love being warm and comfy! Michael Berthold*

- ☐ *Everything! I liked that some days were food related and others were not. Erin Rios*

Kathleen Eckert

We Love October!!!

MONDAY	TUESDAY	WEDNESDAY	THURSDAY	FRIDAY
	01 Don't Sweat It! We Love October!!!	02 Smoothie Delivery	03 Jeans (Color Out Day)	04 PTA Lunch Babes
07 National Chocolate Covered Pretzel Day In Lounge	08 Staff Care Day in 203	09 Treat in Boxes	10 Jeans	11 Fun Time (Campus PD)
14	15 Jeans (House Assembly) Popcorn Delivery to Teachers	16 Cookie Day in Lounge	17 Jeans (Color Out Day)	18 Hour Lunches for Teachers
21 Find the Pumpkins	22 Lunch (Faculty Meeting)	23 Treat in Boxes	24 Jeans	25 Payday Breakfast
28 National Chocolate Day in Lounge	29 Surprise form School Pride & Spirit	30 Smoothie Delivery	31 Jeans & Room Service	

Figure 6.4: We Love October

- ☐ *I love that you made the second longest month of the year, October, a little more bearable and easier to see through to the end. The jeans days were awesome! The treats rocked! I think it was AMAZING overall!!! Kerri Kirk*
- ☐ *Thank you for the surprises. It made coming to work during that hectic month fun. April Shafer*
- ☐ *EVERYTHING!! It really did help me get through the month of October a bit easier when I knew I was getting some kind of treat every day. Brianna Vazquez*

Staff suggestions for We Love February:

- ☐ *Staff volleyball or kickball game the last period of the school day and have students watch.*
- ☐ *Coffee & Hot Chocolate Bar*
- ☐ *Find the Hearts (like find the pumpkins)*

School Transformation Through Teacher Appreciation

- ☐ *Staff Happy Hour*
- ☐ *Notes from students*
- ☐ *Messages written on paper hearts and put in our boxes*
- ☐ *Drawings for class coverage, lunch from a restaurant of your choice, scratch-offs, or Amazon gift cards*

Twitter Challenges

I had the privilege of attending the Principal's Institute with N2Learning a few years ago. A huge takeaway from that experience was, "Who is telling your story?" Schools work to put great things out on social media, but sometimes you need help, so when we are doing certain activities, I like to do a Twitter Challenge with my staff. One example of when I like to do a Twitter Challenge is on Home Visit Day (our teachers visit the homes of all incoming 7th graders the first day they are back on contract in August).

Here is how it works. First come up with a hashtag like #HMSHomeVisits2019. Each time the teachers tweet and use the hashtag their name goes in the drawing. If they tag a media outlet such as a news station their name goes in the drawing twice. I have someone back at the school following the hashtags and putting names in my drawing tub while the teachers are doing their thing. When the event is over, we all gather in the cafeteria for debrief and such. That is when I start drawing names out of my tub and giving out prizes.

Prizes can be gift cards businesses have donated, supplies teachers like such as Flair pens, or anything else you can come up with. The best part is a person's name can be drawn multiple times, meaning they can win multiple prizes.

Kathleen Eckert

Part III:
Recognition

Kathleen Eckert

Chapter Seven
It's the Little Things That Matter Most

Handwritten Personal Notes

When was the last time someone gave you a handwritten note telling you how awesome you are or simply thanking you for doing something for them? Remember how that made you feel? Taking the time to handwrite a note to a staff member is a powerful tool.

I like to keep a folder in our offices and title it Notes. The first thing you need to put in it is a current staff list. This will be used to ensure you write a note for everyone on your staff during the school year. Then as you begin to notice awesome things your staff and teachers are doing you can jot a quick note on a post-it, print off an email, or what method works best for you and put it into the folder.

Approximately every two weeks I pull out the folder and write notes to teachers and staff for the items you have placed in the folder. When I finish writing I highlight the names on the staff list in the folder that I wrote note to. Before I put the folder backup, I look over the staff list and see if there is anyone who is not highlighted that I could write a note to. My goal is to ensure I write a note to everyone on the staff. If you do this process regularly you will write multiple notes to your movers and shakers, and that is not a bad thing.

I also like to handwrite notes to various people in our school district who help us with things. For example, human resources, payroll, finance, and secretaries. It will make their day and they will be very happy to help you again in the future. If you have any extra campus t-shirts, include it with the note. Most people get to wear jeans on Fridays, and this means you will have central office staff supporting your campus.

You could always purchase thank you notes or blank notecards for this but creating a campus postcard and printing them yourself works great and is a lot more cost effective.

There are many ways you can expand on this:
- ☐ Challenge yourself to write every staff member a note first semester and then again, the second semester.
- ☐ Work with local businesses to get coupons donated to include with the notes. Most will give you free item coupons such as ice cream cones, drinks, appetizers, etc.
- ☐ In August, have teachers complete a form, note card, or Google Form that asks what their favorite snack, candy, drink, etc.
  - ☐ Give them their favorite snack or candy with the handwritten note.

Text Messages

I previously shared my strategy for writing personal notes to my staff. One day while writing personal notes and marking them off on the staff list I started thinking. I printed a staff list and decided to track sending out positive text messages to my staff in the morning. I keep the list with my phone charger, so when I unplug it in the morning, I send out a few text messages that say, "Good morning. I appreciate all that you do, and I hope you have a great day!", "I love your heart for your students!", or "I don't know what I would do without you!" Anything that when your staff member sees it first thing in the morning it will start their day off on a very positive note. I only send one or two a day or maybe three to four a week. Use your staff list to highlight who you have sent a morning text message to so you can ensure that you eventually send one to all of your staff member

Wristbands

My first year at Hillwood I was trying to think of a way to recognize students who received all As and Bs for the first semester. While eating with some students in the cafeteria, I noticed some of them were wearing wristbands and a light bulb went off.

I ordered two sets of wristbands. The first ones were yellow and said, "I'm kinda a big deal – Hillwood Middle School", The second ones were navy and said, "I made an impact – Hillwood Middle School". My thought was the student would keep the yellow one and wear it showing others they are a big deal. Then the students would give the navy wristband to someone who has made an impact on their education. I let the students know this could be a teacher at Hillwood, a former school they attended, or simply anyone that has made an impact on them. When the wristbands came in I made a video that was played on our video announcements explaining the plan/process.

When we were ready to roll, we simply set tables up at the front of the cafeteria and students who had all As and Bs for the first semester picked up their wristbands. The effect they had on teachers was simply amazing! Some teachers wore them on their ID lanyard while some wore them on their wrist. The best part was teachers at our feeder schools received wristbands and loved them. The first year we did this a teacher in another district received one of the navy wristbands from a former student. The teacher shared it with her principal, and they did the same thing at her campus.

Tip: When teachers receive a wristband, they can have the student write their name on the inside of the wristband with a Sharpie. That way years from now the teacher will always know who gave them the bracelet.

Bright Spots

A middle school principal in my district shared this idea with me and I ran with it. Every Monday at our administration meeting we share what we saw in classrooms the week before. If we saw something that really stood out the administrator who maintained our bright spot list would add it to the list. A few days before each faculty meeting, I look at the list and tell my secretary how many light bulbs I will need. The first thing we do at faculty meetings are bright spots. I read why someone was nominated for a bright spot, who nominated them, and give the teacher a lightbulb filled with candy. This helps us start all of our faculty meetings off in a positive way.

The second year I did this, some teachers started emailing me things they saw in other teacher's classrooms while they were doing a Husky Holla', (See Chapter 3: Teacher-on-Teacher Walkthroughs).

Hump Day Holla'

My amazing choir director, Jodi Coke, took the initiative and started sending out an email to the staff every Wednesday called Hump Day Holla'. In the email Jodi would recognize 2-4 staff members and talk about something that staff member had done or special qualities that staff member possessed. Periodically her email would start out, "This week's Hump Day Holla' is brought to you by students." For those emails, she would ask students to share with her why they like certain teachers.

Approximately three months into the school year Jodi asked me for an updated staff list. Her goal was to make sure she gave every staff member a shout out during the school year in the Hump Day Holla'.

During the 2019-2020 school year, our instructional coach, Ashley Stroope, joined Jodi to take the Hump Day Holla' to the next level. Jodi put her email out every other Wednesday and Ashley began putting out instructional Hump Day Holla' the opposite weeks of Jodi. The instructional emails highlighted things Ashley saw or heard about happening in classrooms.

Candle of Learning

When I first came to Hillwood, I made it my mission to clean out the storage closets in the school that were filled to the brim with stuff that was

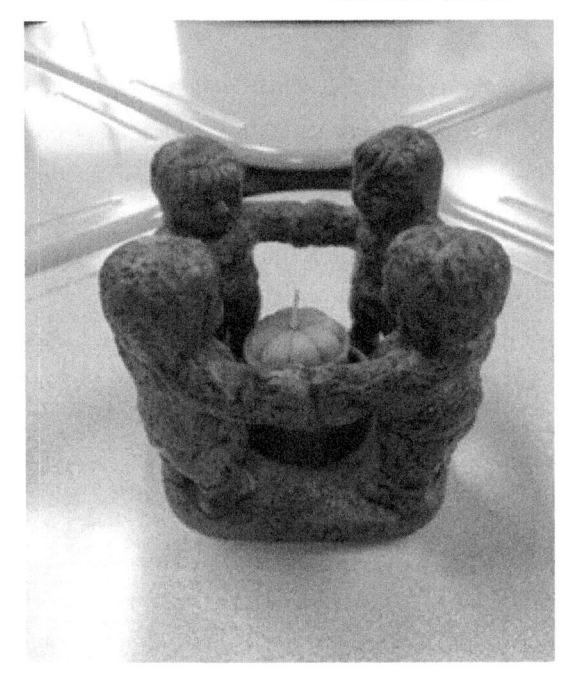

Figure 7.1: The Candle of Learning

simply dumped in a closet. During the cleaning of one of the closets I found an interesting candle (see Figure 7.1).

People said it looks like the Children of the Corn. I decided to keep the candle because I thought I could come up with a fun way to use it. A few months later, the Candle of Learning made its debut. I sent an email out to the staff introducing the Candle of Learning and I gave the candle to a teacher to get it started. The teacher would send out an email to the staff explaining who they are passing the Candle of Learning to and why. After sending the email they take the actual candle to the new recipient. That teacher rejoices with the candle for a few days and follows the same process of passing the candle to another staff member. Here are a few of the emails that have been sent out:

☐ *I am honored Mike Stitt chose to pass the Candle of Learning to me. Mike and friends have made HMS truly feel like home from the day I began*

School Transformation Through Teacher Appreciation

subbing on this campus 8 years ago. I am truly blessed to work with such incredible teachers that I can call my family.

  I would like to pass the Candle to a teacher who ALWAYS goes above and beyond for our staff and students!!! She also happens to be my favorite partner in crime... HEATHER FREEMAN. She is the most dedicated women I know that seeks to serve others. From creative projects like the AVID college fair to running Goodies & Grades for teachers and students to being in charge of Student Council and all those great teacher gifts we get! Somehow she manages all of these big projects while planning 3 preps! She is always on the go and puts in countless hours at school for her students and teacher friends.

  Heather, you are a one of a kind teacher who is truly passionate about your students as individuals. You inspire me daily. I am so thankful for your partnership with AVID and our friendship that has blossomed from this experience together. You are not told thank you enough for all you do so.... THANK YOU from all of us at HMS for ALL the countless things you do to make HMS special. You are appreciated!!!!

☐   Thank you so much to Mrs. Debidart for passing the candle on to me! I am the one who feels truly blessed to get to work with you every day!

  I am passing the candle on to a lady who has been my rock this entire year. She is so calm and professional and everything I want to be when I grow up. Getting up to come to work has been very hard this year, but once I get here I know that there is someone that always makes me smile. She is always there to answer any questions I have and to help me with all of the tough situations that SPED brings. I am sure that she is regretting getting the room with the open wall next to me, but I have enjoyed being her neighbor and friend!

  Thank you so much Mrs. Shaffer! You have literally saved my life this year.

☐   Hello HMS Peeps!

  I would like to thank Todd Nevitt, for the incredible honor and thoughtful words. I thought afterwards......oh great, now I will have to think *of someone to pass it along to. It takes time to carefully plan and select the perfect person to bestow the Candle O' Learning. With that said..........*

It's only been three months since I received this creepy dust collector......AKA Candle O' Learning, but who's counting. Thanks to Lawrence for pointing out I still had the candle in my room, it shed some "light" on the fact that I need to FINALLY pass it along!! I have to admit I was becoming a bit too attached to the candle. Keep the candle for 3 months and you will notice it will start growing on you too!

I choose to pass the Candle O' Learning to Erin Rios. There are so many things that I could say about her. I worked with her for many years, back when she was Walz. She has become a great friend. I have watched her grow in her roles as teacher, wife, and mom. When she is at school, she gives 110% in everything that she does. She is a very organized person which is reflected in how smoothly her classroom runs. She took it upon herself to clean out and organize the Science store room. As a Huddle teacher, she continues to push her students to be successful. I cannot think of a more deserving person.

Love ya Erin!

Todd Nevitt, one of our awesome teachers, took it upon himself to track the movement of the Candle of Learning. When a staff member rejoices in the presence of the Candle of Learning for an extended period of time, he will recep it's movement to the staff. This normally has to be done about once a year.

Teacher of the Month

We have nomination forms available on the wall by the front office, (see Figure 7.2). Students simply pick up a form, fill it out, and put it on my door. Once a month the administration team goes through the nominations and selects the teacher of the month, and my secretary orders the plaque.

The day of our pep rally I send a note to the student(s) who nominated the teacher and ask them to meet me on the side wall before the pep rally begins. These students don't know why they are meeting me. Just before the

School Transformation Through Teacher Appreciation

pep rally starts, I let them know the person they nominated has been selected as the teacher of the month. The students join me in the middle of the gym floor when it is time to present the award. I read what the student(s) wrote on the nomination form to the crowd. Then I say, "Our teacher of the month is," put the microphone in front of the student(s), and they announce the teacher's name. Then the student(s) present the teacher with the plaque and nomination form(s).

Once the pep rally is over, I put the other nomination forms for teachers who were not selected that month in the teacher's boxes. The first year I threw them away, but then I realized if I put them in the teacher's box it is a great little way to make them feel loved. We did discuss making the nomination process digital a few times, but I love the power of the handwritten nomination forms. (During the fun time of COVID, we did go digital with the nomination forms and printed them all out to put into teacher mailboxes,)

It is important to make sure the students know the teacher is selected by what they write on the nomination form as the reason(s) why they nominated the teacher, not by the number of nominations turned in for a teacher. Periodically a group of students will get together and about twenty will nominate the same teacher, but not put a reason why. Some students have written letters as to why a teacher should be the teacher of the month. In the end, it is simply fun reading what the students write.

In order to share the wealth, I do keep track of when a teacher receives teacher of the month and work to ensure there are a few years between a teacher getting it for a second time.

Tip: Use a staff list to keep track of what teachers received what awards and the date they received it. I track Above and Beyond, Teacher of the Month,

TEACHER OF THE MONTH

```
Name of Teacher: _____

Your Name: _____

Date: _____
Please share the reason/reasons why the teacher is being recommended for
Teacher of the Month:
```

Figure 7.2: Teacher of the Month Nomination Form

and Husky Heart on the same sheet. I use this to help ensure we are sharing the wealth among our staff instead of the same teachers getting all of the awards.

Above and Beyond Award

Horace Mann wanted to provide two crystal apple awards a year to our school, (see Chapter 4: Insurance Companies). As I reflected on how I wanted to utilize these awards I decided to call it the Above and Beyond Award. The administration team and counselors discuss who they feel truly goes above and beyond but may not get the recognition they deserve. Then the award is presented to the teacher at a pep rally by the Horace Mann representative and myself.

Husky Heart Award

At the end of the end of each school year schools have award ceremonies. While these are designed for students it is also a great way to recognize a few staff you feel need a little recognition. So, I created the Husky

Figure 7.3: Above and Beyond Award

Heart Award. Due to the size of our school, we have two award ceremonies, one per grade level. One Husky Heart Award is given during the 7th grade ceremony, and one is given during the 8th grade ceremony. There is basically no criteria for this. I like to look for staff members who have a huge impact on our school and need a little recognition. (See Figure 7.4)

Jeans

One of the BEST ways to reward staff is with jeans! It is free and they are relaxing. Personally, I am more likely to get down on the floor with students when I am in jeans instead of a skirt. We, of course, have the standard jeans on Fridays with a school shirt, but here are a few more ways you can use jeans to show appreciation or thanks to your staff.

For this first one, keep in mind I live in Texas. It is VERY rare that we have days below 30 degrees. But my staff knows if the temperature is below 30 degrees, it is an automatic jeans day for the campus. I always hear

Figure 7.4: Husky Heart Award

stories about Facebook posts and text chains blowing up when someone sees the temperature is below 30 degrees. My teachers get really excited for cold days and when it is that cold outside, who doesn't want to dress comfy?

A few years ago, we had what we called a stranger danger incident. Someone tried to get a student to get into their van about a block from the school. So we asked for volunteers to be outside before and after school the week of an incident. The first three days the weather was great, then the next two days it was below 20 degrees. I could see the headlines, "School no longer cares now that it is freezing outside." So, I sent out an email that said if a teacher volunteered those two days, they got their choice of a Sonic drink (picked up at 9 am) or a jeans pass. We had over twenty teachers monitoring outside along the street before and after school those days. Please know lots of my teachers would have done this simply because they love kids, but the added incentive never hurts. Plus, I only had to buy one Sonic drink.

Set up a Remind 101 account for your staff or some other form of a group text. About two or three times a semester I send out a text in the evening telling them to wear jeans tomorrow. Sometimes I play with it and have a little fun by tying it to a staff member. For instance, when our local NFL team, the Dallas Cowboys, made the playoffs a teacher asked me if they could wear jeans and Dallas Cowboys shirts or jerseys. In the Remind I said, "Jason Agee has requested a jean day tomorrow with a Dallas Cowboy shirt or Dallas Cowboy colors. Enjoy!"

Sweats

When I first came to Hillwood the only sweats days were during the Twelve Days of Christmas, but the staff really looked forward to that one day a year, (See Chapter 9: Twelve Days of Christmas). A few years ago, we had more than normal going on and pulling everyone in different directions. I sent out a Remind saying, "Don't SWEAT it! We got this!" The first time I sent something like this I explained they get to wear sweats. Now about two or three times a year I will send out "Don't SWEAT it" Remind. Every time I do I get lots of thank you texts and emails. My staff really loves these surprise days.

Hour Lunches

At my campus we have a total of four lunches, two per grade level. Once a month we have hour lunches. On those days all 7th graders eat one lunch, and all 8th graders eat one lunch. Students are allowed to stay in the cafeteria or go outside to our football field. On these days teachers get a 30-minute lunch and then they monitor students outside for the other 30 minutes.

As a reward for Technology Badging, (See Chapter 3: Tech Badging), the department who has earned the most badges each month got to have an hour lunch, meaning they did not have to do their 30 minutes of duty. A few of the departments really started working to get the hour lunch, so like I tend to do, I began to think bigger.

Educators are very competitive by nature, but sometimes they just need a little incentive. When we were competing against other middle schools to see who could raise the most money for the Desert Storm War Memorial, I told the teachers if we won, they would get a week of hour lunches. This means administrators and counselors would have to monitor the students during the hour lunches. This was such a powerful incentive to our teachers that we actually tripled the amount raised by the other middle schools.

Due to the popularity of teachers coveting their hour lunch we have now incorporated them into our We Love October and We Love February, (See Chapter 6: Make It Fun).

Warning: When you give all teachers the hour lunch it is important to plan it when all of your administrators and counselors are on campus and make sure they are all outside on that day. For us this means eight adults for 600 plus students, but it works for us.

Tip: Try to schedule your teacher hour lunches close to payday. It is a lot of fun listening to them plan where they are going to lunch that day and you want to make sure they have the money to fully enjoy their lunch.

Staff Shoutout Board

When we had a new addition added to our building, we ended up with an extra six-foot white board. A teacher on our teacher cadre, Amanda Steelman, said, "Why don't we hang it in the teacher's lounge and put a bunch of dry erase markers with it. Then people could give shout outs to anyone they want." We immediately made arrangements to have the white board hung up. The teacher printed letters on various colors of paper that spelled out Staff Shoutouts and put them on the top of the board. Staff members love doing shoutouts on the board and those who the shout outs are about love it even more. (See Figure 7.5)

Figure 7.5: Staff Shoutout Board

Scratch Offs

An elementary principal in our district posted on Twitter a picture of a scratch off ticket she made for her teachers. I instantly fell in love with the thought and contacted her. She told me that she made the cards and bought stickers from Amazon that turn the cards into scratch offs.

Using Microsoft, I made business card size scratch offs with our school logo. I put the following prizes on the scratch offs: Jeans Pass, Sweats Pass, Super Sonic (I would pay for their Super Sonic Wednesday), Class Covered (they just needed to coordinate it with an administrator or counselor), Teacher Supplies (a bag full or random fun supplies), and Gift Card (there were very few of these since they cost money). (See Figure 7.6)

Figure 7.6: Scratch Offs

    I first shared the scratch offs with my teachers at an October professional development session. At the end of each session the teachers each got a scratch off. They loved them. From there the plan was to have the administration team periodically do mass class visits looking for something. For instance, teachers not sitting at their desk. When the administrator went in the room if the teacher was up moving around, they were left a scratch off.

    During the 2017-2018 school year, our district began to focus on substitute fill rates and teacher attendance. Where we have never had a major issue with substitute fill rates and our teachers always get their absences put into the system in a timely manner, I simply just listened when the district talked about this issue. Once or twice, I thought about trying to do something for teachers with perfect attendance, but then financial reality would sit in. I simply did not have funds to do something for all of my teachers who have perfect attendance. And let's face it, their name simply going into a drawing

Figure 7.7: Perfect Attendance

for a prize such as a gift card is not a true motivator or reward unless they are the one who wins the gift card.

About six weeks later was when I learned about the scratch offs and started working on them. Then it came to me: at faculty meetings each month, I can give a scratch off ticket to each teacher that had perfect attendance the month before. Gwynn Christmas, one of my teachers, loves to get a scratch off for perfect attendance so much she will actually debate if an absence is worth losing a scratch off.

During COVID our faculty meetings were conducted via Zoom, so I started putting the perfect attendance scratch offs in the staff boxes. (See Figure 7.7)

Warm Fuzzies

I heard about a secret society that does various things when I was touring a college campus. I immediately emailed myself a quick reminder to play around with this idea. About a year later, I found these little pom poms with eyes called Warm Fuzzies. I ordered two tubs of the Warm Fuzzies and continued to ponder how I wanted to use them.

After the Warm Fuzzies came in they sat on a shelf in my office for a few weeks. One day as I was leaving my office to do walk-throughs, I grabbed them and took them with me. I stopped by a teacher's room and shared with her that I would like to start a secret group of teachers and students who randomly recognize our staff for the great things they do. The teacher loved the idea and said she would love to take on this task. (See Figure 7.8)

We discussed that she would take on the task or pass it to another teacher, but basically, I would not know. The hope was to truly create a secret society of people to recognize staff. We decided that whoever is over the Warm Fuzzies would simply leave a note in my box when they need me to order more Warm Fuzzies. I would purchase them and leave them on a shelf in my office. They would come by and pick them up at some point when I am not in my office.

Figure 7.8: Warm Fuzzies

School Transformation Through Teacher Appreciation

Treat	Saying
Almond Joy	Thanks for adding "Joy" to a child's life!
Animal Crackers	This place would be a zoo without you!
Apple	What's worse than finding a worm in your apple? Finding half a worm in your apple!
Baby Ruth	Keep on batting for students!
Can of Soda	Thank you for your CAN do attitude!
Cheez-its	You're the "cheeziest"!
Chips	You're all that and a bag of chips!
Cookies	You're such a smart "cookie"!
Cookies	What do the cookie and computer have in common? They both have chips!
Cracker Jacks	Why was the Math book sad? It has a lot of problems!
Dark Skittles or Dark Chocolate	Feed your dark side!
Dum-Dum	You're no Dum-Dum Thanks for sharing your knowledge!
Extra Gum	You are EXTRA amazing!
Extra Gum	Thanks for going the "extra" mile!
Fast Break or Kit Kat	You deserve a "break" today!
Gardetto's	You deserve a snack break!
Gold Fish or Swedish Fish	You are O'FISH'ally awesome!
Gold Fish	Why are fish so smart? They are always in Schools!
Hershey	You're worth your weight in chocolate!
Jolly Rancher	Thanks for being so "jolly"!
Junior Mints	Thank you for your commit "Mint" to students!
M & M's	You are Magnificent and Marvelous!
M & M's	Why did the blonde get fired from the M & M plant? She was throwing out the W's!
Milky Way	You're a star in our galaxy!
Mounds	We appreciate the "Mounds" of work you do!
Nestle Crunch	You are always helpful in a "Crunch"!
Nestle Crunch	When it is CRUNCH time, we want you on our side!
Peanuts	We're nuts about you!
Rice Krispie Treats	"Snap, Crackle, Pop" we think you're really tops!
Rice Krispie Treats	Thanks for putting "Snap, Crackle, and Pop" into Hillwood!
Snickers	You never "Snicker" at a child's needs!
Snickers	You are not you when you are hungry!
Starburst	You're a star!
Starburst	Bursting to tell you - You Are Amazing!
Strawberry Fruit Snacks	Why were the little strawberries upset? Their parents were in a jam!
Tootsie Pop	It's time to rock & roll! You've got this!
Trail Mix	Trail Mix is just M & M's with obstacles!
Twix	Who doesn't like chocolate and caramel with a cookie crunch?
Twix	Nothing comes TWIX me and my chocolate!
Whoppers	Thanks for a "whopper" of a good job!

Figure 7.9: Teacher Treats

Teacher Treats

Most of us have seen or heard about putting catchy sentences on candy bars and such and putting them in teacher's boxes. Figure 7.9 are some I have used in the past:

If you don't have the money to purchase items, try partnering with the company that supplies your campus vending machines or contact local stores for donations.

Class Cover Thank You

Like most schools, we sometimes do not get enough substitutes to cover when teachers are out. We are very lucky that our district will pay teachers to cover other classes during their conference period. Due to that we usually get our classes covered when we are short substitutes. But there are times we have unfilled positions and teachers don't volunteer. For those times I have a list where teachers are listed by what periods they have a conference. I look at the list and either text or call the teacher and ask them if they will cover the class, we need coverage for. Now, I am not stupid. I know my teachers are a LOT more likely to agree to cover when I reach out than when my sub coordinator reaches out. That is why I do it. Because of that I track who covers when I ask so I don't ask them more than other teachers. Within a few days they will get a bright orange piece of paper that says thank you for helping me cover classes with a scratch off taped to it. These teachers still get paid to cover the class, but because I had to ask them, I like to do a little something extra as a thank you for their support.

Chapter Eight
Value Them as a Person

Staff Beginning of Year Google Form

Each year the campus secretary has teachers fill out a hard copy of their updated information such as address, emergency contact, etc. One year I told her we were going electronic, and I was going to add additional information that I wanted to know. The following items were added:
- ☐ Kids' Names and Ages
- ☐ Favorite Candy
- ☐ Favorite Sonic Drink
- ☐ Favorite Snack

I added the kids' names and ages because I feel that in order to value your staff as people you need to know about their most prized possession(s). When staff is asked about their kids they light up and it lets them know you care about them as a person, not just as a teacher or staff member.

For favorite candy, sonic drink, and snack I print the list out by teacher and keep it in my Notes folder, (See Chapter 7: Handwritten Notes). Sometimes when I write teachers notes or simply want to thank them for something I refer to the list to make sure I get them something they enjoy.

Staff Notes for Me

Currently I have a staff of over 120 and I am getting older. Those two things combined means I can forget things. This is especially true when I am in work mode and get tunnel vision going. One day I realized when a teacher tells me something about their personal life they are going through, I would write on a post it notes to follow up with them and I started getting a stack of post it notes. Having the reminder to follow up is a great idea, but it was doing me no good when I was out walking the building and talking to staff.

With this in mind, I loaded my staff list into a Google Sheet and then set that Google Sheet as an icon or app on my phone's home screen. I put all of my post-it note reminders into the Google Sheet.

I like to walk the building before school starts a few days a week. This is a time that I am able to just chat with staff and check in on them. With my Google Sheet I can pull it up really quick before entering a teacher's room. Before this when I saw a teacher I would simply ask, "How are you doing?" Now with my new system I can ask, "How is your dad doing?" or "How is Alayna doing at Texas Tech?" This has been a game changer for me and talking with my staff on a more personal level.

Notecards Home

Bear with me for a minute on this one. Every year we print mailing labels for all of the parents of students at Hillwood. These labels are printed by teams. The labels are placed in our PD room along with note cards that have our school logo on them. The plan is for each teacher to write approximately five to ten note cards a month to parents about their student and drop them in our outgoing mail bin. The mailing labels are used to let the teachers know which parents have not received a note yet. By the end of the school year every parent will receive a note card about their student from one of their teachers.

I have put this strategy under Value Them as a Person because the responses from the parents are awesome. Many parents email the teacher with…

☐ *Hi Ms. Robinson,*

We received your note about Kyler recently, and I just wanted to take a moment to let you know how much we appreciated the gesture. It is not often that a teacher takes the time out of their extremely busy schedule to acknowledge one of their students by sending a handwritten note to the parents. It was very thoughtful of you, and it speaks volumes about how much you care

School Transformation Through Teacher Appreciation

for your students and demonstrates the high level of passion you have for teaching.

We have long known Kyler to be a leader and a kind and respectful young man (although we are just a tad bit biased in that regard, LOL), but to hear it from one of his teachers is one of the best compliments a parent can get. We are glad you are enjoying having him in your class and are more than happy to share him with you and Hillwood MS.

Thank you again for your kind note...it most definitely brightened our day! Todd & Meaghan Wallace

- *I just wanted to let you know we received your sweet note in the mail about Quentin and are so appreciative to hear your kind words about our son. Middle school can be a rough transition and as parents we really encourage him to advocate for himself which means that I don't hear from his teachers very much. I really appreciate you taking time to send us a note letting us know he is doing well. He absolutely loves science and your class is definitely his favorite.*

  Thank you,
  Erin

- *I received your note over the weekend and it really made me smile to read it. Thank you so much for letting me know that she's doing better and is more focused. I try to keep her motivated and sometimes it's hard. I really appreciate you reaching out to me and I appreciate all that you do for my daughter. Have an amazing spring break! Also, we were going to leave and maybe go out of town tomorrow, would she be missing anything if she was not in class? I'm debating on if we will just wait until the school day ends. Thank you.*

- Figure 8.1 is a note one of my teacher's received in the mail from a parent. As you see, even though this is something designed for the students and parents, many times our parents are so genuinely touched by receiving the notecard in the mail they reach out and thank our teachers.

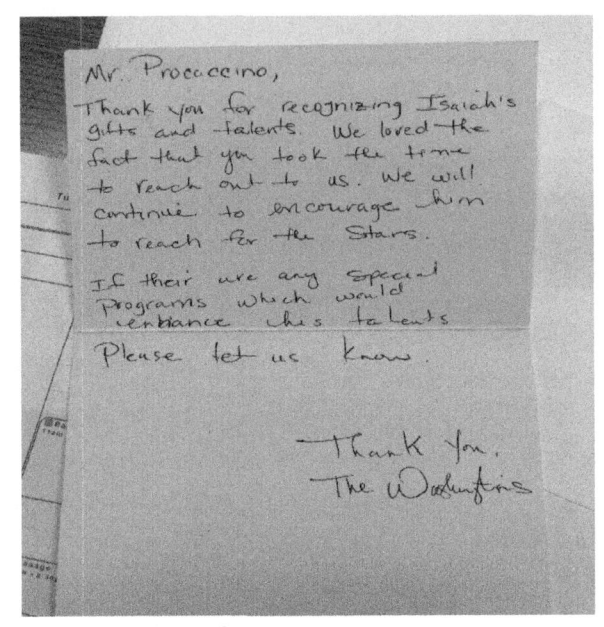

Figure 8.1: Note from a Parent

Teacher Appreciation Week

Make it your goal to blow Teacher Appreciation Week out of the water! Your teachers will appreciate it and you will have a lot of fun doing so. With this in mind you need to do something every day of the week, even if it is a simple gesture. Here are a few suggestions:
- ☐ Partner with your campus student groups such as STUCO, NJHS, AVID, etc. Have the students from those groups plan breakfast, snacks, or a desert bar for the teachers. The students can decorate the teacher's lounge and the students bring the food needed.
- ☐ Partner with your PTA. Our amazing PTA provides lunch one of the days as well as gift baskets we can use as prizes for drawings or games.
- ☐ All campuses have staff that work the front counter. Most of the time that counter is hopping, and those staff members stay busy. But they also go through random down times. Starting in January have them start contacting community businesses to ask for donations for teacher

appreciation week. We have received lots of great things by simply asking. Coupons, gift cards, items we can give away, food or snacks, and various other things. My office staff goes and picks up the items when they can, and we keep them in a particular location. Then the week before we look at what we have received and make a plan. Sometimes we fix up little bags with coupons and candy for all teachers and sometimes we do games or drawings for the items. The past two years we have received enough items that we did daily drawings on the PA for teachers every day. The teachers did not know it, but by the end of the week every teacher's name is called as a winner over the PA (the students really get into this as well). Once you establish partnerships with your community businesses, the process goes a lot smoother.

Tip: Keep a spreadsheet with the business name, contact person, contact info, and what they donated. Then the following year, this is where you start.

Below are one of our Teacher Appreciation Weeks outlines. I like to spread everything out. Now this is my plan, so only myself and the office staff helping me see this list. We don't actually send this out to the teachers. But we have started sending out rhymes the day before thanks to our resident GT wordsmith, Mike Stitt. This allows teachers to know if breakfast, lunch, or snacks might be provided the next day so they can plan accordingly.

- ☐ Teacher Appreciation Week
    - ☐ Monday
        - ☐ Breakfast from AVID & STUCO
        - ☐ #WhyITeach Quotes posted
        - ☐ Drawings
    - ☐ Tuesday
        - ☐ HMS Lunch
        - ☐ Subway Cookies
        - ☐ Drawings

- [ ] Wednesday
    - [ ] HMS gifts & cards
    - [ ] Cupcakes
    - [ ] Drawings
- [ ] Thursday
    - [ ] PTA Lunch – On the Border
    - [ ] Spring Creek BBQ Gift Certificate
    - [ ] Drawing
- [ ] Friday
    - [ ] Shipley's Donuts
    - [ ] PTA gift
    - [ ] Coupon bags
    - [ ] Drawings

When it comes to planning the teacher appreciation gift from the school, I put a lot of thought and planning into it. We are very limited financially, so I am always trying to think of gifts that are special and meaningful.

Teacher Appreciation Gift - Something Nice

We are limited on what we can spend school money on for staff, so I started trying to think of teacher appreciation gifts that are meaningful and inexpensive. One day, my dad forwarded me an email that talked about how a 4th grade teacher had students write down something nice about each student in the class and the teacher took those and created a list for each student of what their classmates said about them. The email went on to talk about how one student carried that list in their wallet throughout their life and the impact it had on that person. This got my wheels spinning.

In November, I gave each staff member a staff list and told them to say something nice about each staff member. I went on to say if they don't know a person they need to go meet them and then list something nice for them.

Knowing this would take a while, I asked them to return the list to me by the beginning of January. When some questioned what it is for I told them to simply chalk it up to the method behind my madness.

I did get a couple of staff who felt this was too much, so I told them to do what they could. I then sent an email to the staff letting them know my goal was not to stress anyone out. If they feel it is too much for them just do what they can. Ironically, when I sent that email out, multiple people replied with things like, "Tell them to suck it up, they have four weeks," and "Why wouldn't we want to say nice things about our co-workers". Those emails reaffirmed for me that I might be onto something with this plan.

As the lists were turned in, I had an office staff member who compiled the comments in a spreadsheet by teacher name of who the comment was about. This did take a while, so I made sure this staff member had a few months to work on this part. Once everything was inputted in the master spreadsheet, it was turned over to our registrar, Cynthia King. Cynthia then used the spreadsheet to create a Wordle for each staff member with the comments their co-workers said about them. Cynthia printed them on linen paper that was a school color and put them in cheap plastic frames I bought, (see Figure 8.2).

Then during Teacher Appreciation Week in May, each teacher was given their framed Wordle. The looks on the staff's faces was simply amazing! I loved listening to teachers saying who they thought wrote what and there were tears.

This is a very impactful and inexpensive gift. The key to this is you have to start early to give each step of the process plenty of time.

Teacher Appreciation Gift - Thank You Book from Students

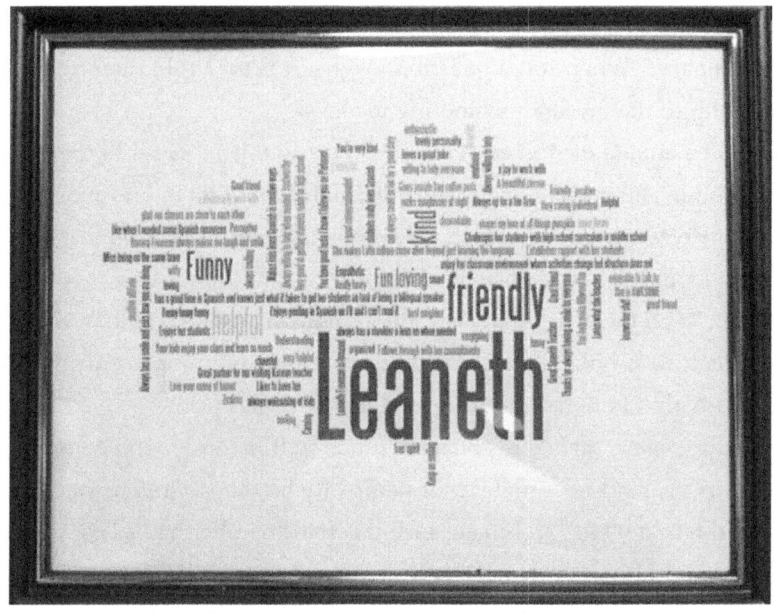

Figure 8.2: Something Nice

    This idea came about when I saw the binding machine at the school that had not been used for years. I spent a few days trying to think of "how" I could use it to do something for the teachers. After contemplating it a while an idea hit me. I was going to make each teacher a spiral bound book of letters and notes from their students.

    I partnered with my substitute coordinator and got the plan rolling in October. When a sub would check in, my sub coordinator would look at her list of teachers to see if she had had a sub for that teacher since she started the project. If the teacher had not, she would give the sub a sheet with directions on it as well as some blank copy paper. The direction sheet told the sub to give each student a piece of copy paper and read them the following:

> *Mrs. Eckert wants you to help her celebrate the amazing teachers here at Hillwood. Please take a few minutes to use the piece of paper I gave you to write a note or letter to (teacher's name the sub was substituting for). All of the letters will be bound in a book and given to the teachers during Teacher*

Appreciation Week. This is a surprise, so please do not mention this to the teachers.

The direction sheet went on to tell the sub to turn in the direction sheet and letters/notes from the students to the sub coordinator at the end of the day.

The sub coordinator printed each teacher's name on card stock along with Teacher Appreciation 2014-2015 to use as the cover. She would bind the cover, notes, and another piece of cardstock as the back cover. Once she had a teacher completed, she locked it up in a cabinet and marked them off of her list.

As May was approaching, we had about five teachers we did not have books for. So, I emailed them and set up a day I could be in each of their classes for the first 20 minutes. I told the teacher they would find out later what I was up to and I swore the students to secrecy.

The books were later given to each teacher as their teacher appreciation gift from the school. This was another very impactful and inexpensive gift.

Teacher Appreciation Gift - Letter from a Loved One

In October I put together a 9 x 12 envelope for each teacher. Each envelope consisted of:

- ☐ Standard mailing label on the front outside with the teacher's first and last name.
- ☐ Larger label on the front that said:
  - ☐ Do not open this envelope. Give it to a loved one and tell them not to tell you what is inside.
- ☐ Inside the envelope:
  - ☐ Direction sheet, (see Figure 8.3)
  - ☐ Blank copy paper.
  - ☐ Envelope addressed to myself with a stamp on it and a standard mailing label with the teacher's first and last name on the back.

KELLER INDEPENDENT SCHOOL DISTRICT
HILLWOOD MIDDLE SCHOOL

The Hillwood Middle School community is dedicated to developing students into self-confident, highly educated, and well-rounded individuals.

8250 Parkwood Hill Blvd.   Kathleen Eckert, Principal
Fort Worth, Texas 76137
Phone: 817-744-3350
www.kellerisd.net

Hello,

Please do not share this or anything about it with the person who gave you the envelope.

Directions:
- I would like you to write a letter to your loved one that gave you this envelope. The grand plan is for me to give your letter to your loved one during Teacher Appreciation Week in the spring.
- If you need help getting started think about:
  - What do you love about them?
  - What makes this person special?
  - How have they made you proud?
  - Why are they in education?
  - How have they impacted your life?
  - How have they impacted the lives around them?
- There is paper in the envelope for you or feel free to use any paper you want.
- After you write your letter please put it in the enclosed, stamped envelope and send it to me.
  - Your letter will remained sealed in the return envelope until it is given to your loved one.
  - I have written your loved ones name on the back of the stamped envelope so I know who it is for.

I appreciate your help making Teacher Appreciation 2017 special for our Hillwood family. If you have any questions please feel free to contact me at Kathleen.Eckert@KellerISD.net

Sincerely,

Kathleen Eckert, Principal

Our vision: An exceptional district in which to learn, work, and live.   Intentionally Exceptional

---

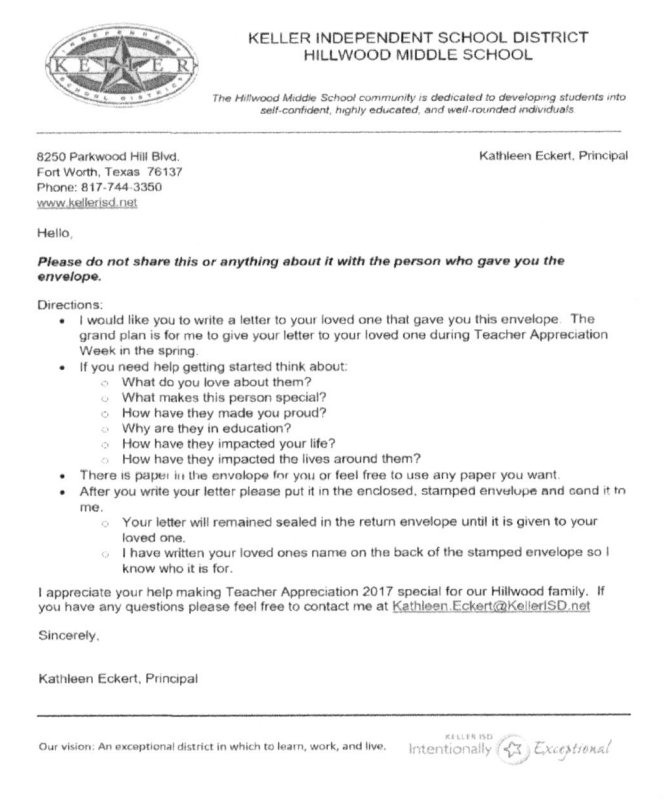

Figure 8.3: Directions for Letter from a Loved One

At the November faculty meeting each teacher and staff member were given their sealed envelope and instructed to give it to a loved one. Within a week I started getting a few envelopes in the mail. By March I had received about half of the letters from the staff's loved ones. So, I decided to put a staff list outside my door and highlighted the names of who I have received something for. I explained the list to the staff without telling them why or what it was. As I received letters, I would highlight the teacher's name. By

Figure 8.4: Student Putting Notes in Bag of Notes

May, I had a letter for all but two staff members. I wrote a letter for the two I did not have a letter for.

During Teacher Appreciation Week, the letters were given to the teachers. As I was delivering them, Coach Pulis came running down the hallway after me. She was crying and said she had not made it through the first few lines yet, but this was the best gift ever.

Teacher Appreciation Gift - Bag of Notes

At the beginning of the year teachers decorated a bag. At the front of the room, I had white handled gift bags along with ribbon, letter stickers, character and object stickers, ribbon, glitter glue, markers, and map pencils. The teachers were told to decorate a bag. The only requirement was that I needed their last name on the bag.

At the end of the day, I gathered the bags and put them in a closet. Once that was done, I ordered index cards in a variety of shapes and sizes, and I had office aides die cut various shapes on cardstock.

Once a month I took the teacher bags to the cafeteria along with the notecards, die cut shapes, markers, and pens. I spread the bags out on the stage by grade level and department and put the other supplies on a table at the front of the cafeteria. Students were then asked to write notes to any teacher or staff member they would like. I had administrators, counselors, office staff, etc. make bags as well. After writing their notes, the students put them in the appropriate teacher's bag.

I did this 6-7 times during the course of the year. (See Figure 8.4) After the last round I got a few trusted students to skim through the notes in each bag to make sure there were not any negative notes. (These are middle school students.) Then during Teacher Appreciation Week, the bags were given to the teachers as their gift from Hillwood.

Teacher Appreciation Gift - Student Videos

I asked my audio-visual teacher, Todd Nevitt, if he thought he could make a video for each teacher with current and former students telling individual teachers what they thought of them. Once he agreed we came up with four different ways/times to video students.

- ☐ We established a day when there was no school so former students could come make videos at Hillwood in Mr. Nevitt's studio. An email was sent to former students who were currently attending Central High School, the school we feed into.
- ☐ We set a day Todd and a crew of his current students would go to Central High School and video students during lunches.
- ☐ We had Central High School email their current students and parents with the dates for the first two days we would be videoing during student lunches along with directions of how they could make their own video and send it to Todd.

Once videos were gathered Todd created an AV class project where the students would edit the videos and combine them into videos for each individual teacher. Then during Teacher Appreciation Week, Todd emailed each teacher their gift from the school.

Candy Bouquets

Each summer I have teachers who give up time for various reasons such as leadership team planning day, department planning time, staff development planning, etc. One year I decided I wanted to thank and recognize those teachers in August when the entire staff was back together for the first time to get ready for the new school year. I had the idea of using blue (school color) solo cups with Styrofoam and sticks to make cute candy bouquets for each teacher.

The original plan was to use a piece of green Styrofoam that is used for flower arrangements, small kabob sticks and full-size candy bars. It did not work. They were simply too top heavy when we glued the candy bar to the sticks.

I brainstormed with my secretary to try and come up with an idea to make this work. We started by gluing the candy bars on the sticks and giving them a day to dry. The plan was five full size candy bars per cup. Then we ended up getting rocks from the school yard and putting some in the bottom of the cup and spraying foam sealant we bought from Home Depot on top of the rocks in the cups. Before the foam hardened, we put the candy sticks in the foam.

In August I had about 20 candy bouquets and in front of the staff I thanked individuals and told them why I was thanking them. Then they came to the front to collect their candy bouquet to the applause of their co-workers.

What wish can I grant for you?

The first year that we had house bashes, the house committee wanted teachers to volunteer to work at the house bash for their house as house bashes are after school. In a faculty meeting the house committee shared what the house bashes would look like and what they need teachers for. After I expressed that it is 100% optional for them to work the house bashes, but if they decided they wanted to work I asked them, "What wish can I grant for you?" I gathered their input in a Google Form. Then after each house bash I granted their wishes if they attended. Many said they did not need anything in exchange for attending. Those who said they wanted something kept it very reasonable such as jeans pass, sweats pass, or Sonic drink.

Staff Care Day

My amazing counselors started this. A few days out of the year, they take over our professional development room and turn it into a staff care day area. They dim the lights, play soft music, and sometimes put a virtual fireplace on the pull-down screen. The staff can sit and relax or participate in various activities the counselor has out. Activities include painting rocks, coloring adult color pages, or play with kinetic sand. The counselors also set out infused water and light snacks.

Appreciation Time

About 2-3 times a year I send a text out to the staff in the evening saying, "It's Appreciation Time." Staff is to email or text a staff member they have not talked to or texted in the past two weeks and tell them why you appreciate them. They need to copy me on the email or send me a screenshot of the text by 6:30 am the following day. If they do this, they can wear jeans that day.

Every time I do this, reading what my staff tells each other makes my heart warm and sometimes they make me laugh. Here are a few examples:

☐ From Kelsie Bass:
Hi Shelton,

School Transformation Through Teacher Appreciation

Just want you to know that I am so blessed to work with you! You are always so kind, well dressed, and despite everything you're keeping up with away from school- you always have a smile on your face.

I look forward to another awesome school year of teaching with you! And many more selfies!

☐ From Tobie Vaughn:

Mrs. Whorton,

From day 1, you have been the most sincere and loving person. You have been welcoming and helpful, and I know that there will be great laughter anytime we cross paths. I am beyond grateful for that. Thank you for all that you do.

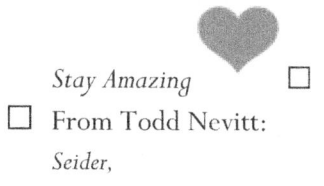

Stay Amazing ♥ ☐

☐ From Todd Nevitt:

Seider,

I still don't understand why you left me. Was it something I did? Something I said? Something I didn't do or say? I still can't get used to not seeing you across the hall from me everyday, your short stature alleviated as you sit perched on a tall stack of adirondack chairs. I was really privileged to work across the hall from you for a couple of years, watching you make ELA exciting and building great relationships with kids. You're great at what you do and your students love to come to your class everyday because of your energy and sense of humor. I just hope you'll come back to the 500 hallway someday. I can change. I promise. I know I've said it before, but this time will be different.

Warmest regards,

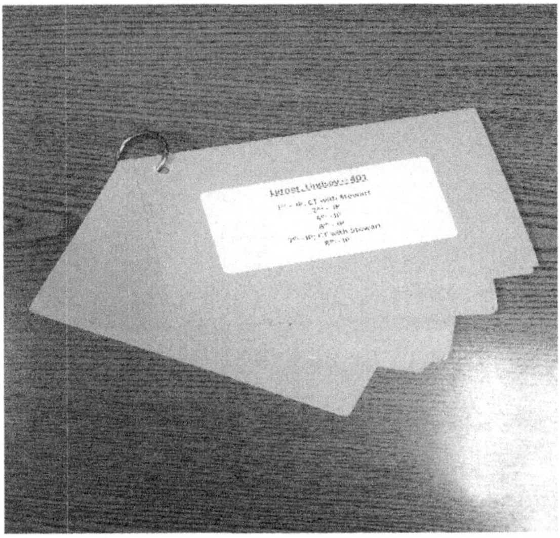

Figure 8.5: Walk Through Ring

TAG Walkthroughs

Every year I create five walkthrough rings. Each ring has its own color of index cards, and the teachers are distributed out on the various rings (see Figure 8.5). Between the administrators and the instructional coaches, I have five people who do walkthroughs. To start we each, take a ring and have two weeks to conduct a walkthrough on every teacher on the ring. After we do the walkthrough, on the back of the index card we put the date, class period, and our initials. At the end of the two weeks, we switch rings.

Jaci Harvey, one of my assistant principals, suggested we TAG out with the teacher and teach/run their class for 10-15 minutes instead of doing a walkthrough. The teachers loved it.

Chapter Nine
Miscellaneous

Super Sonic Wednesday

I got this idea from a principal friend, Melanie Stitt. We partner with a Sonic location close to our campus to get 44-ounce fountain drinks for .99 plus tax. Then on Wednesdays the teachers can pay $1.50 to the front office and fill out the form in Figure 9.1. Our office ladies gather the money, call in the order, and pick it up. (Tip: 2 four pack drink holders fit great in a case of paper box.) The Sonic location writes on the cup what each drink is. Student office aides help unload the drinks from the office staff's car and put them on our back counter. The students tape the filled-out forms to the top of each drink and arrange them in order of the teacher's classrooms. Next, they put them on a cart and deliver them.

This is a great way to put a smile on your staff's face and it does not cost you a thing. The office lady that does the pickup keeps the change from the orders. After taxes each drink costs $1.07, so they keep the extra .43. The first year we did this the office ladies let the money build up. At the end of the year, they each had about $100.

For us Super Sonic Wednesday happens EVERY Wednesday, no matter what is going on, including state testing. On state testing days the office staff gets the drink ready for delivery and I deliver the drinks to the teachers myself. It is a great way to help me be visible during state assessments.

Funny Memes

I was at an elementary school one day and in the teacher restroom they had a few funny comics up on the wall. This was around the time that Memes were on the rise. The next day I was walking through the front office

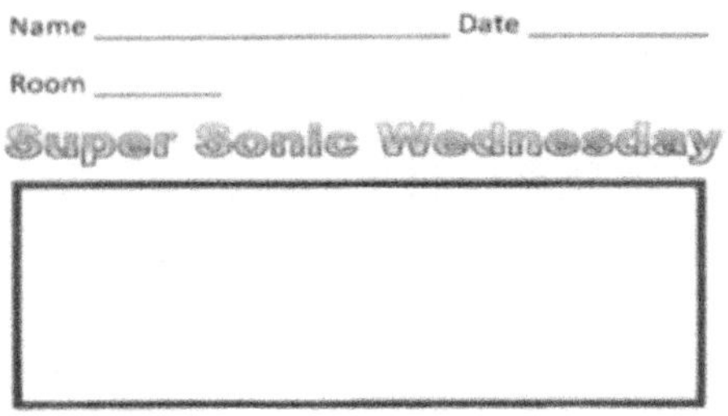

```
Name _____ Date _____
Room _____
```
Super Sonic Wednesday

[   ]

Figure 9.1: Super Sonic Wednesday Slip

and saw office aides sitting at a table with nothing to do. Then a lightbulb went off. I talked to Glenda Taylor, one of our front office ladies, and formulated a plan. Glenda would have students look up funny teacher related Memes, Glenda would print and laminate them, and then the office aides would hang them in the faculty restrooms around the school. To start, students put 2-3 per restroom. Then every month office aides would hang up new ones and take down the old ones. I knew we were onto something when I found a teacher coming out of a faculty restroom and she looked at me and said, "It's new Meme Day. I need to go check all of the restrooms."

Baby Betting Pool

My first year at Hillwood we had eleven babies born to staff members. It felt like we were having baby showers all the time. I decided to try and have some fun with trying to guess who was expecting. For this to work it is vital that the expecting parent only tell you they are expecting and that they hold off on posting on social media and such. So, when a staff member tells me that they or their spouse is expecting I ask them if they want to do a baby betting pool. If they do, we work together to set up the dates of the baby betting pool. Sometimes parents want to wait until after the first trimester or they want to shout it from the rooftops immediately. Once we set the dates we get going.

School Transformation Through Teacher Appreciation

Baby Betting Pool

- Opens Monday, Oct. 27 and Closes at 8:00 am on Thursday, Oct. 31.
- The goal is to bet on who you think the expecting parent is.
    - For each $1 you bet on the correct expecting parent you will receive a jeans pass.

    OR

    - For each $2 you bet on the correct expecting parent you will receive a sweats pass.
    - You can place multiple bets on the same person. Once the expecting parent is announced Eckert will ask you if you want jeans, sweats, or a mixture of both.
    - All money raised goes to the expecting parent.
- How do you place bets?
    - Give cash to Nurse Kim or Nurse Pat.
        - Write your bets on the poster by writing your name by who you think is the expecting parent and how much you are betting on them.
    - Venmo @Kceckert
        - Show Nurse Kim or Nurse Pat your Venmo.
        - Write your bets on the poster by writing your name by who you think is the expecting parent and how much you are betting on them.
- If you are asked if it is you, please play along. This allows the pool for the expecting parent to increase.
- Please do not discuss with students or get them involved.
- Hint: It is not Butcher, Phillips, or deBidart.

Figure 9.2: Baby Betting Pool Directions

A staff list is enlarged and printed on poster paper and taped to an easel and our nurse decorates the easel with baby stuff. Then I send the information in Figure 9.2 to the staff in an email.

When we first started doing the Baby Betting Pool, we only did jean passes. We started incorporating sweats passes about five years later.

On average we raise $100 for the expecting parent. The fun part is when the grapevine fires up. The Baby Betting Pool becomes the talk of the campus for the 3 or 4 days we open it. One of the best pools we had was when one teacher really played it up. She sent out an email looking for saltine crackers and would make little comments about not feeling well. In that pool only $1 was placed on the actual expecting parent.

Baby Betting Pool 2.0

The Baby Betting Pool worked great when we only had a few pregnancies a year. During the 2019-2020 school year we broke our previous record of eleven babies with our new record of twelve babies. With that many pregnancies guessing the expecting parent became interesting. The Baby Betting Pool 2.0 was started thanks to Meredith Akers. The following rules and plan were sent out to the staff in an email.

Baby Betting Pool 2.0 opens Tuesday, Jan. 21 and closes at the end of the day Friday, Jan. 24.

- *These pools will be for 5 parents, (all money raised will be divided evenly):*
    - *Kayleigh Nelson - ELA*
    - *Brittany Pulis - ELA*
    - *Ashley Stroope - Instructional Coach*
    - *Zach Woolhouse - Band*
    - *Matt Stephens - Band*
- *There are 3 ways to Bet/Win with 2.0:*
    - *Gender - Boy or Girl (Nelson & Stephens have announced their gender, so no gender betting on those two)*
        - *$1 with a $5 max.*
        - *Jeans pass for each $1 bet on the correct gender.*
        - *Passes given once the parents announce the gender.*

School Transformation Through Teacher Appreciation

- Birthdate
  - $1 per date you guess. Max $5 per date you guess.
    - Can guess multiple dates.
  - This is the actual birthdate, not due date.
  - 2 scratch-offs for correct guesses.
- Birth Time
  - $1 per time you guess, (hour and minute).
  - This is the actual time the baby is born.
  - The person who gets closest to the actual time gets a $20 Tropical Smoothie gift card.

The posters are up outside of the Nurses Office, (see attached picture). You can pay Nurse Kim cash, or you can Venmo me and show your Venmo to Nurse Kim. Write your last name with your bets.

Pay to wear jeans and sweats for January will be added to the money collected from the Betting Pool.

With the number of parents, we were collecting for I decided to add pay to wear days for jeans and sweats to the pool money. For those days I will send out a Remind the night before saying jeans for $1 and sweats for $2. I did this about 5 times during the pool.

Easter Egg Hunt

I was seeing the various ads about Easter egg hunts and the wheels started spinning in my head. How much fun would it be to have a staff Easter egg hunt? So, I went to local stores and asked them to donate fillable plastic eggs. After I had about 300-400 eggs, I started filling them with various gags items as well as fun items. Some of the things we filled the eggs with were:

- ☐ Jeans passes
- ☐ Candy
- ☐ Money – change and a few bills
- ☐ Paper clips
- ☐ Shaving cream

- ☐ Notes with sayings like "You are Awesome"
- ☐ Gift cards
- ☐ Free items from local stores/restaurants

Leading up to the hunt the staff was told they must have an Easter Basket to participate in the hunt. No grocery bags and such.

    The day of the hunt, I got several athletes who were in the last class of the day to hide the eggs. They loved the thought of hiding them for the teachers. Once school was out and duties were completed the teachers lined up outside the gate of the football field. The best part for me was seeing Brian Ketcham and Coach Nelson waiting outside of the field with Easter baskets waiting to play. Once all participants were there, we opened the gate. It was hilarious watching our staff run around the football field looking for eggs.

Tips: Don't put chocolate in the eggs if it is hot outside. The eggs were hidden for about an hour before our hunt and we are in Texas. The eggs with chocolate in them ended up a melted mess. Also, the hunt itself is over very quickly. Ours was done within 10 minutes.

Easter Egg Hunt 2.0

    I loved the Easter Egg Hunt but wanted to think of a way to make it last longer, so Easter Egg Hunt 2.0 was started. Heather Sims was the brainchild behind the new version. Heather got 30 plastic fillable eggs and wrote a number on the outside of each egg. The number correlated to a prize on the table in her office. The best part was inside the egg was a piece of paper that told the staff member "how" they had to come to the office to collect their prize. For instance: skip, bunny hop, ice skate, grapevine, etc. Then the eggs were hidden throughout the school. As teachers found the egg, they would open it and come to the office in the manner stated in the egg to claim their prize. Prizes included small gift cards, spring flower seeds, Easter items, etc.

Bonus: We like to pull video footage of the teachers coming to the office ice skating, skipping, and such and include it in our year end video or simply to email out to the staff as something fun.

Mentor Thank You

A fellow principal shared this idea with me. Each year she would give her mentor teachers a small thank you for mentoring new teachers. She would give them a gift card to Subway with the letter in Figure 9.3.

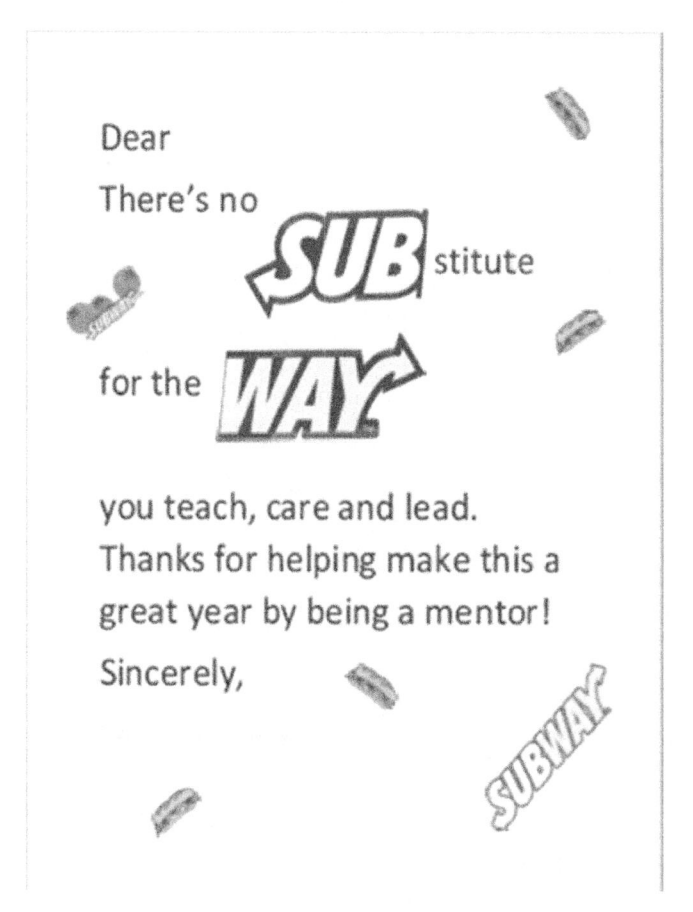

Dear

There's no SUBstitute

for the WAY

you teach, care and lead.
Thanks for helping make this a great year by being a mentor!
Sincerely,

Figure 9.3: Mentor Thank You

Chair Massages

Several years ago, a masseuse, Rebecca, reached out to us and asked if she could do chair massages for the staff. The first time Rebecca came the staff signed up for 15-minute time slots and she did the massages for free. The staff enjoyed the massages, so we set up for Rebecca to start coming once a month. Rebecca sent a link to the staff where they could sign up for a 10-minute massage for $10 or a 15-minute massage for $15.

Rebecca's appointments filled up fast. So, the next year she started coming twice a month and then the next year she started coming weekly. To say our staff loves Rebecca would be an understatement.

If you can find a masseuse that can come, do chair massages for your staff I highly recommend it. It is amazing how relaxing a 15-minute massage can be, especially in the middle of the school day.

End of Year Ice Cream Social

The last day of school for students is normally an early release day for us. I like to have an ice cream social after the students leave. In the cafeteria we have two lines set up with everything you can imagine making your favorite bowl of ice cream. Once all the staff has their ice cream, we watch the end of year staff picture show created by Lynn Shelton (see Chapter 9: Shelton's Picture Show), celebrate retirements, give out district service pins, and do some fun awards. The time is designed as a celebration for the year, and it is a great way to wrap it up.

Shelton's Picture Show

One of our teachers, Lynn Shelton, is known for always taking pictures. From the first day of school to the last Lynn is always taking pictures of students and staff. For the end of year, he puts together a picture show of staff pictures from the year and puts it to music. The staff loves seeing memories from the year. There are always laughs, but I am always surprised at how excited the staff gets at seeing their picture in the show.

Fun Awards

One year I had our PALS class create funny awards for the teachers. Once they created a list of awards, they had the students vote on which teacher should get each award. Our PALS then presented the awards with a token gift at our ice cream social. Some examples of awards and gifts were:
- [ ] Best dressed - clothing item from a thrift store
- [ ] Best hair - went to a coach who shaved his head, and they gave him turtle wax

The key is the categories and gifts were completely created by students.

Twelve Days of Christmas

This is not a new or innovative idea, but it is one that everyone seems to enjoy. For the Twelve Days of Christmas, you start by seeing what the twelve school days before the Christmas break are and then coming up with a theme for each day. Our fabulous Heather Sims takes the Twelve Days to a whole new level and creates fun little rhymes for each of the days. She creates new rhymes each year. Here is a set of her rhymes:

Day 12

Twas' 12 days before break and all through the school,
Teachers were weary, kids were actin' a fool.
What in the world could help us not feel so grumpy and mean,
Why I think what is needed is a little caffeine!
Head to the lounge for coffees or teas,
Hot cocoa might be more your speed,
And of course, any fixins' you could possibly need.
You're loved and appreciated for all you do,
So, for the next 12 days, we'll celebrate you!!!

Day 11

It's Day 11 and Friday to boot,
We think a contest would be a hoot!
Who can build the best gingerbread house is the task?
What's the winning prize you might ask?

Well for this one bragging rights will be about it,
But try hard, have some fun, and don't be a (ahem) twit.
Enough for everyone, no need to scrounge
All the supplies will be in the lounge,
Happy Friday!!!!

Day 10
Saw Santa this weekend, oh what a sight.
He told me what would make Day 10 just right.
"Extra, Extra," he said with a wink and a nod.
"Wow" I thought, "the old man's a bit odd."
But then I realized what extra must mean,
Why an extra day of Sonic and I get to wear jeans!!!
So put on those blues, bring your dolla' fifty,
A day of extras will be quite nifty!
(Disclaimer – drink orders must be into Glenda by 9:30)

Day 9
Day 9 brings you a salty treat,
Chips, chips, and more chips to eat.
Come down to the lounge for today's yummy snack,
But for pete's sake, try not to smack!!!

Day 8
Day 8 is the day some like the best.
It's the day we give our waistbands a rest.
No zippers to zip, but let's not get drastic,
Wear your sweats today and enjoy the elastic!
#formerlyknownaswindpantWednesday

Day 7
There are 7 more days that we all will meet.
It's round two of chips and snacks that are salty!
Today we've added sweet, don't want to be faulty
Come get a little and then come back later for more.

School Transformation Through Teacher Appreciation

Day 7 is round two of chips and snacks that are salty,
but we've added in some sweet, don't wanna be faulty!
Variety is the key to the spice of this day,
to help keep your Thursday bah humbugs at bay!

Day 6
Day 6 is special and maybe a bit messy,
But it's ok, on Friday no one is dressy.
A chocolate fountain with good stuff to dip,
However, it would be bad manners to take a big sip.
So come on down and fix a plate,
Of sweetness that tastes oh so great!

Day 5
Chocolate, strawberry, cake, and twist
Day 5 brings donuts; you get the gist.
Not sure what else I can say
What more do you need to start your day?
 Other than glazed yummy goodness in your belly
There's plenty for all, no need to be jelly!

Day 4
Fruits are sweet,
Fruits are yummy,
Fruits are good for more than your tummy.
Something healthy is the midst of the junk
Day 4 won't grow your Badunkadunk.

Day 3
Day 3 is awesome and that's no lie,
There's no need for lunches to bring or to buy.
Come down tomorrow to the faculty meeting,
The boss will have a feast for us to be eating.
As if a great lunch weren't quite enough,
There's one more treat on this day of good stuff.
The weather's been weird, but what else is new?

A little extra comfort would be such a coup.
Let's wear sweats one more day!
That's enough to make us shout "hooray"!

The kids are crazy and running wild,
And what's up with this weather, way too mild.
I know it's not cold, but it would be nice to be comfy.
A bonus day of sweats

Day 2
Day 2 means we're getting so close to the end,
A good start to the day will help us attend.
Come down to the lounge for breakfast delight
PTA is providing us with this morning bite!
7:45 is the beginning time,
For a nosh and fellowship-truly sublime.
But that's not all for some of our folks,
Team meetings are cancelled and that's no joke!
Now if this isn't for you, please don't be sore.
Instead thank your stars you don't teach a core!

Day 1
Day 1 is here, time for celebration
The train can now leave from Crazy Station.
The kids will go home, and we will too,
My wish for peace and joy for each of you!
The CP is gone, the goodies are done.
But I can't resist a little more fun.
Names will be drawn for a prize or two,
Maybe the lucky winner will be you!
As our 12 days draws to an end,
To you all good wishes I extend.
Enjoy the holiday and get some rest,
Because when you get back, I'll be ready for some tests!!!

School Transformation Through Teacher Appreciation

If you decide to do the Twelve Days of Christmas, you can do some amazing things with little things. If you are on a budget incorporate jean days, sweat days, and Super Sonic days.

Find the Penguin

During the final week of school before the holiday break, we have a fun round of Find the Penguin. Our penguin is a plastic tree ornament. The penguin is hidden somewhere in the school each day and hints are sent out to the staff periodically until the penguin is found. When a staff member finds the penguin, they bring it to the office to claim their prize.

For the prizes we partner with our PTA, and they create some amazing, themed gift baskets. Normally the value of the gift baskets is about $30-$50, but a few years ago we had a mom that wanted to blow the lid off of the gift baskets. She started a few months in advance getting gift certificates donated. Her themed baskets were valued at $100 easily. We were blown away.

A few years ago, we took it up a notch and had Coach Stitt create the hints. Coach Stitt is a diabolical and gifted-talented wordsmith. His clues make you want to bang your head on the wall, but when you hear where the penguin was hidden the lightbulb goes off.

Convocation Shirts

Several school districts have a big kick of celebration to start the new school year. Our district calls our kickoff convocation. Like most staff we are slightly competitive and want to show our school spirit. With that in mind, we like to wear matching school shirts. Normally the teachers have to pay for their shirt, or we have to see if PTA will pay for them.

There are many other ways you can get staff shirts paid for such as grants, law offices, dentist offices, doctors, etc. Some are simply willing to pay for them and others would like to have their business name on the shirts. Either way, free is free and the staff appreciate it.

Get to Know Each Other Cards

Create a set of cards that you can pull out periodically to help your staff mingle and learn more about each other. These can be used as a quick "get to know you" activity, as a station in professional development rotations, etc. Here are some sample questions you can put on the cards:

- ☐ If you could relive one year of your life, what year would it be? Why?
- ☐ What person from history would you have enjoyed knowing? Why?
- ☐ What is your favorite TV show? What do you like about it?
- ☐ If you could have an article published in a popular magazine, what would be the subject?
- ☐ Name two people who have encouraged you sometime in your life.
- ☐ What is something you have never done that you would like to try?
- ☐ What was your favorite story as a child and why did you like it?
- ☐ Share something no one knows about you.
- ☐ What is something you want people to remember about you?
- ☐ What school subject has been most difficult for you? Why?
- ☐ If you could make a law that people would live by, what would it be?
- ☐ If you designed a bumper sticker, what would it say?
- ☐ Open discussion

Reach Out to Parents for Help

We all have some parents who want to help, but simply don't know how. One thing you can do is find out if you have any parents who own local businesses. We have an awesome parent who owns Shipley's Donuts. She provides donuts to our staff twice a year and in return we put a thank you to her business on our school marque.

Another great source is to ask if anyone works for airline companies. We do a lot of things where students need earbuds. If I was to purchase them using school funds, I would have to use an approved vendor and most cost a minimum of $10 a pair. On an airline flight, my husband had a fantastic idea.

School Transformation Through Teacher Appreciation

He suggested I work with parents who work for airline companies to get some of the free earbuds they give out on flights donated to the school.

I have noticed that when I request specific items in my weekly parent email, I get a larger response than if I just ask for help. When we were first starting to use technology regularly, I sent out an email to parents asking if they worked for a company that might be upgrading their technology and would donate their old items to the school. One parent brought us 40 computer monitors that enabled us to set up a lot of teachers with double screens. Another great thing to ask for are Keurigs. I put in my weekly email that we were looking for some gently used Keurigs for the teacher's lounge. Within three hours of the email going out we had 3 used and 7 new Keurigs with lots of pods.

Parents want to help!

Secret Pal

My first few years I organized secret pal for those who wanted to participate. The last several years our choir director, Jodi Coke, has taken over organizing secret pals. Basically, if you want to participate you get your secret pal something worth about $5-$10 a month and then you reveal yourself at the end of the year. We all know it is nice to get a little surprise every once in a while, and this is a great way to do it.

School Gift Certificate or Check

Many principals have constraints on what they can buy for teachers, but they can buy things for teacher's classrooms and/or students. I got this idea from my mentor, Steven Johnson. You make up gift certificates from the school to give out as prizes to teachers. (See Figure 9.4) I like to give these out when we do various competitions at the start of school or during professional development. Tip: Put an expiration date on the certificate, especially if you are using your budget money and have to spend it by a set deadline.

HMS Olympics 2016
Gift Certificate

This certificate entitles
to $50 to purchase items for your classroom

Authorized by

Not redeemable for cash. Redemption value not to exceed $00.00

Expires May 1, 2018

Figure 9.4: School Gift Certificate or Check

Holiday Cards

Every year we try to think of a fun theme for our staff holiday card. From reenacting the tongue on the frozen pole from A Christmas Story (see Figure 9.5) to getting creative with Elf on the Shelf (see Figure 9.6) to coming up with a holiday card COVID style (see Figure 9.7), the staff who participate in the holiday card enjoy the small treat of being a part of the card. At first, I would come up with ideas, but eventually decided to capitalize on staff to come up with ideas.

Figure 9.5: A Christmas Story Staff Holiday Card

School Transformation Through Teacher Appreciation

Figure 9.6: Elf on the Shelf Staff Holiday Card

Figure 9.7: COVID Staff Holiday Card

Team Building Activities During Professional Development

My first year at Hillwood when I mentioned team building activities, the first thing I heard from one of my administrators was, "We don't want to put our shoes in a pile." That told me they wanted fun activities, not warm and fuzzy activities. With that in mind I incorporate some type of team building activities or games into all full day professional development days. From creative activities like magic carpet races across the cafeteria floor to traditional favorites like musical chairs, teachers simply want to have fun. If creating team building activities is not your cup of tea, consider doing a carnival (see Chapter 6: Make It Fun).

At least once a year I like to do a quick survey of teachers to grab personal info from them. Sometimes I use this info and sometimes I don't, but it is great to have when you want to toss together a quick activity.

Payday Breakfast

Payday Breakfast is an idea I got from my mentor, Steven Johnson. The idea is a designated group of staff members provide breakfast for the staff on payday. (See Figure 9.8) For the first breakfast of the year I like to have the administration team sponsor it. After the first month I divide the remaining months up by department, and in recent years I started dividing the remaining months up by houses. I assign one of the office ladies the duty of payday breakfast reminders. Glenda Taylor e-mails the group providing breakfast a reminder email about a week before.

People have done and brought a variety of items. Some use electric skillets to make bacon or pancakes, some bring casseroles, and some swing by the donut shop. We normally have a small variety of items each month, but the main benefit of payday breakfast is staff fellowship. I love walking into the teacher's lounge on these days to see a large portion of my staff eating breakfast together and socializing.

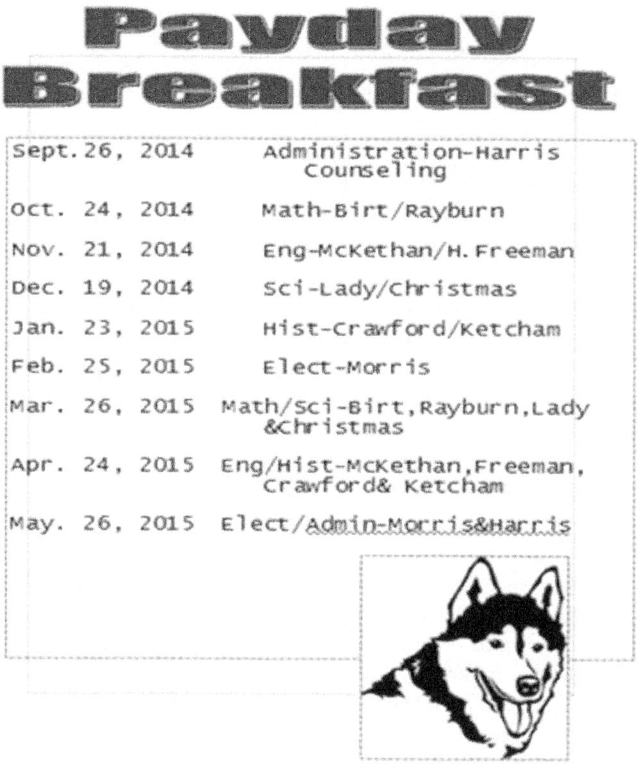

School Transformation Through Teacher Appreciation

Payday Breakfast

Sept. 26, 2014	Administration-Harris Counseling
Oct. 24, 2014	Math-Birt/Rayburn
Nov. 21, 2014	Eng-McKethan/H. Freeman
Dec. 19, 2014	Sci-Lady/Christmas
Jan. 23, 2015	Hist-Crawford/Ketcham
Feb. 25, 2015	Elect-Morris
Mar. 26, 2015	Math/Sci-Birt, Rayburn, Lady &Christmas
Apr. 24, 2015	Eng/Hist-McKethan, Freeman, Crawford& Ketcham
May. 26, 2015	Elect/Admin-Morris&Harris

Figure 9.8: Payday Breakfast

Popcorn in the Teacher's Lounge

This quick and easy idea was already in place at Hillwood when I joined the campus. Every Monday and Friday the front office pops popcorn and it is left in the lounge for the day for staff members to eat.

Birthday Wall

Our staff has come close to doubling in the nine years I have been at Hillwood. We actually have more students and staff than some high schools in neighboring districts. Due to this, one of my staff members, Jennifer Paxton, asked me if she could create a wall in our teachers' lounge of staff and their pictures. Previously, when I was visiting an elementary classroom, I shared that the teacher had created a birthday wall in her classroom of her students. I asked Jennifer what she thought of combining the two ideas and creating a birthday wall in our lounge with staff pictures. I already had all of the staff's birthdays from our beginning of year Google Form, (see Chapter 7: Handwritten Personal Notes) Jennifer immediately emailed the staff and requested them to send her a picture. With the help of her beautiful daughters, our Birthday Wall was created. When you look at figure 9.9 in the bottom right corner you can see where Jennifer created an index for the wall in staff alphabetical order. The index includes what they teach and their room number.

Figure 9.9: Staff Birthday Wall

Birthday Cakes

Each month, two cakes are placed in the teacher's lounge and a list of birthdays for the month are sent out to the staff. I mean who doesn't love a piece of cake on a long day?

Snacks on State Testing Days

We all hate state testing days. From test security to proctoring it is simply a pain. A great way to break the tediousness is to have snacks set up in the lounge for the staff. If you are on a budget buy fruit, veggies, and snacks from a warehouse type store. This will allow you to stretch your money. Then have an office lady cut up the fruit and veggies and replenish as needed during the day. Teachers love this! They go get a plate or bowl of munchie stuff and take it back to their testing site.

Potluck

My first few years at Hillwood we had a staff holiday party somewhere off campus in the evening. Since the holidays are so busy not all of our staff would be able to make it. Meanwhile, our last day of school before the holiday break is a half day for the students, so we started doing a potluck for the staff.

You need to have one main organizer for this. For us, that is Heather Sims. Heather has teachers sign up to bring a side dish or desert. Then on the day of, teachers drop everything off in the teacher's lounge. While the teachers are teaching, Heather gets everything set up in the cafeteria. Then once the teachers have cleared the building of students, they go hangout and eat in the cafeteria.

In addition to eating, Heather always plans a few games for staff to participate in and/or has a staff video for everyone to watch while they eat.

Chili & Soup Cookoff

Who doesn't like to brag if they make a mean pot of chili or soup? This is perfect for cold months. Set up a signup list in advance so people can sign up to bring a pot of chili or soup. From the list, you can pre-make name tents that tell what is in the pot and assign it a number for voting. The staff member's name is not on the tent, so voting is done anonymously. Staff members who don't want to bring a dish, but want to participate can sign up to bring crackers, cheese, bowls, spoons, etc.

On the day of, we have tables lined up in the teacher's lounge with lots of power strips. Staff drop off their crock pots in the morning. We have an administrator who is over our cookoff. The administrator arranges the crockpots and puts out the premade name tents. A ballot box is set up with voter forms and pens on a separate table.

During lunches, teachers sample and eat. At the end of their lunch, they cast their vote in the ballot box. After all lunches have eaten and voted, the administrator tallies the votes. The winner is announced via email or over the PA and they get to house the Cookoff Trophy until the next cookoff.

Room Service

Inspiration for ideas is literally everywhere if you take the time to look and reflect. This one came to me when I was staying in a hotel room at a conference. I decided to use three categories for our room services with various options under each category: sweet, salty, drink. After determining what items, I wanted to list under each category I had a parent volunteer type it up on half a sheet of cardstock, laminate it, and tie a piece of twine to the top of it to use as a door hanger (see Figure 9.10). Tip: On the door hanger, teachers were told they could only select one item from each category.

Two days before room service, the door hangers were put in teacher boxes, and they were asked to use dry erase markers to mark their selections and have them hanging on their classroom door on the set day.

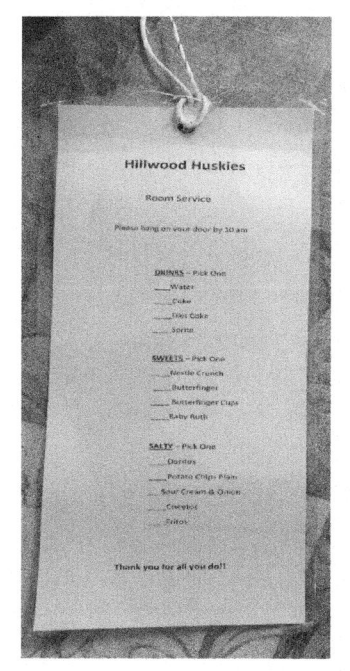

Figure 9.10: Room Service Door Hanger Card

On the day of, I grabbed a few students to help me. We had a few ice chests with drinks on one cart and the snacks on another cart. There were four of us working. Each would take the teacher's hanger off of their door, collect the items they selected, put the door hanger in a basket we used to collect them, and take the teacher's requested items to them in their classroom.

The teachers loved it! The only thing to take into consideration is you need enough of the items you listed on the door hanger to ensure you don't run out. This means you will have lots of extra items left.

Root Beer Floats

I have not done this, but we had a realtor do this for our staff. They set up everything on a cart and decorated it with their logo. Then they hit the halls and went class to class offering to make staff a float.

Happy Cart

This is a staff favorite. On a cart, I put big plastic bowls, like the party size you can get from Walmart cheap. Then I put various snacks in each bowl such as cheese balls, pretzels, gummy bears, animal crackers, trail mix, etc. Each bowl has a ladle. I push the cart to the classroom, ask the teacher if they want anything off of the Happy Cart and hand them a small bowl. The teacher uses the ladles to get what they want. (See Figure 9.11)

Sometimes I have an ice chest with drinks in it as part of the happy cart. When I do this, I have a student help me. They love to miss class for little things like this.

Figure 9.11: Happy Cart

Tie in National Days

When we do, We Love October and We Love February, I like to tie in national days when I can. This includes National Homemade Soup Day, National Bubble Gum Day, etc. If you are looking for ideas this is a great way to find some. I simply Googled national days for October, and lots came up. There really is a day for everything.

Wheel of Winning

I had one of my engineering classes build me a spinning wheel with a whiteboard finish. (See Figure 9.12) It is amazing! I pull it out during events where we are all together as a staff. If someone wins whatever game we are playing, they get to spin the wheel of winning. On the wheel, I write various items they could win. Normally, half of them are stupid like high-five

Figure 9.12: Wheel of Winning

someone, etc. I try to think of funny things to put on the wheel in addition to actual prizes such as gift cards.

In August 2020, we played various games during our professional development week. On the wheel I had four spots with various gift cards. On the other spots I had hand sanitizer, Clorox wipes, and a face mask. If they landed on one of these, I would simply tell them to go grab it out of the supply closet. It was hilarious to watch them spin and chant for no more hand sanitizer.

Parking Spots

This idea came from an elementary school, but I tweaked it to fit our needs. An elementary school in our district allows teachers to buy parking spots and paint them. Then that spot belonged to that teacher for the remainder of the school year. They used the money collected to make a college scholarship for former students.

I immediately fell in love with the idea, but I decided to put the money collected into our Sunshine account so I could buy gift cards for the staff. The parking spots cost $40 for a school year and painted their parking spot. (See Figure 9.13) Each year this gives me about $600 for gift cards to use during the school year for staff.

Random Acts of Kindness Bingo

As part of We Love February (see Chapter 6: Make It Fun), I thought it would be fun to do bingo. I shared my thoughts with Heather Sims and she immediately asked if she could do it. Since she is so amazing and I will never turn down help, I said "heck yeah!"

Heather created a nine square bingo, printed it on bright paper, and put it in teacher boxes with a Kind bar. Teachers have three days to complete all of the tasks on their bingo card and turn it into Heather. All bingo cards turned in were put into a drawing and the winner received a small gift card.

Figure 9.13: Staff Parking Spots

Take a few moments and look at figure 9.14. Let's say only half of your staff decided to participate. Think about the impact the random acts of kindness would have with just part of your staff participating. From students to staff, this fun idea will have a positive impact.

Justin Timberlake Video

Heather Sims had the idea for our administrators and counselors to dress up as certain roles that are depicted in Justin Timberlake's video for Can't Stop the Feeling. Heather recruited our district video department to help with her idea. Here is the outcome: https://youtu.be/dDjTNaAfU8c

Random Acts of Kindness Bingo

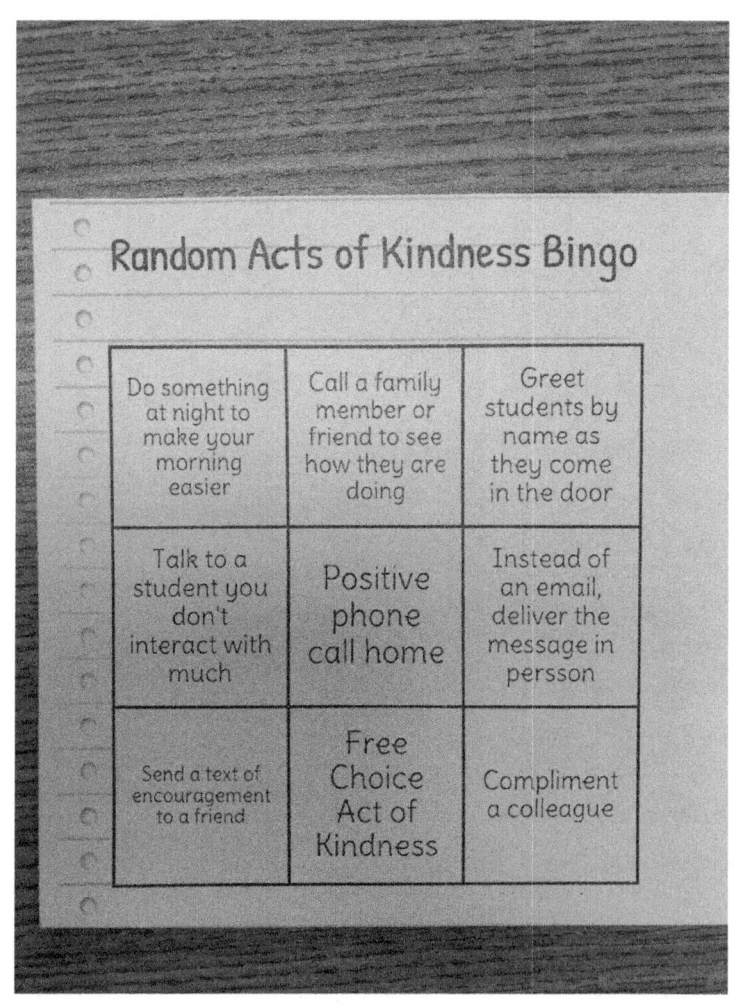

Do something at night to make your morning easier	Call a family member or friend to see how they are doing	Greet students by name as they come in the door
Talk to a student you don't interact with much	Positive phone call home	Instead of an email, deliver the message in persson
Send a text of encouragement to a friend	Free Choice Act of Kindness	Compliment a colleague

Figure 9.14: Random Acts of Kindness Bingo Card

We originally filmed it in 2016 and shared it with the staff at a faculty meeting in November. Before playing the video, I told the staff the admin team has a little treat for them. They loved it and laughed through the video.

In the fall of 2020, I decided to send the video out again to the staff. Of the eight of the team that were in the video, six were still at Hillwood. The staff loved it.

King or Queen of the School

I honestly don't remember where I got this idea, but it is a lot of fun for the students and teachers. Every year in February or March it is time to determine the new King or Queen of Hillwood. In a nutshell, the students buy die cut hearts (February) or shamrocks (March) for fifty cents. Then they give the heart or shamrock to who they think should be King or Queen of Hillwood. The staff member with the most hearts or shamrocks at the end of the week is announced and crowned at a pep rally.

Our teacher over announcements, Todd Nevitt, is always making references that he wants to be the King of Hillwood. He does this periodically during the year and really ramps it up on the daily video announcements the week before and the week of the sales. This helps get the students excited about the week.

Just selling the hearts or shamrocks is not enough. The teachers have to get into it as well. Normally we have about twenty teachers that go all out to get hearts or shamrocks. They do so because of bragging rights, but also because of the incentives offered. Each year the incentives vary based on what gift cards I have. Normally I do a mix of gift cards and scratch offs. As I am writing this, it just came to me that I could use a School Gift Certificate as a prize for this (See Chapter 9: School Gift Certificate). Hmmm...next year.

Each year we raise about $1000 doing the King or Queen of Hillwood. All money raised is put into our YES account to help pay for supplies for the program (See Chapter 1: If You Don't Have the Money Find It).

Find the Memes

This is a fun spin on our yearly Easter Egg Hunt (see Chapter 9: Easter Egg Hunt) that I did during Teacher Appreciation Week. I found 50 Teacher Memes, printed them, and cut them out. On the back of each Meme, I wrote a number that correlated to a prize in the conference room. When the teachers found a Meme, they claimed their prize and taped the Meme to the

Figure 9.15: Memes from Find the Memes

window outside of my office (see Figure 9.15). I left the Memes up for a few weeks so staff could stop by and read them if they wanted.

Chapter Ten
Don't Forget Your Substitutes

It seems like the pool of available substitutes just keeps getting smaller and smaller. We combat this by doing little things to appreciate our subs.

Remind for Jeans and Special Days

Have your sub coordinator set up a Remind (text) account for subs. Make sure to include all subs that come on your campus. A few days before any special days occur, have your sub coordinator put out a Remind telling all subs what will be happening at your school on certain days. For example: *Tropical Smoothie for lunch Friday at Hillwood.*

Having a Remind set up is great for jean days and dress up days. Subs love to participate if they know.

Give Them a School Shirt for Jean Days

This one seems simple but is often not thought of. Give your substitutes a school shirt they can wear on Fridays or jean days. Some suggestions of where to get shirts would be extra convocation shirts, student groups, and athletics. If you are at an elementary campus, reach out to the middle school and high school you feed into. They can ask their student groups and coaches for a few extra shirts for you.

Sub of the Month

Figure out a way to recognize your substitutes. Sub of the month is a great way to do this. You can pick a sub to recognize or do a monthly drawing where every time they sub at your campus their name goes in the bin. There are lots of ways to recognize them. Certificate, email to the staff, celebrate them at a pep rally, etc. The point is to make them feel special and want to come back to your school.

Super Sonic Free on Wednesday

Earlier you read about Super Sonic Wednesdays. On those days I buy drinks for the subs. I normally hit the ATM every few months and give money to my sub coordinator. On Wednesdays she will offer them a drink. If they order one she uses the money I have given her to pay for it. Most of our subs don't order a drink, but they feel special because it is offered.

Coffee Pods, Water, and Chocolate as They Check In

We keep a Keurig with pods and Styrofoam cups along with bottled water and chocolate in our sub check in area. Our coordinator makes sure they know those items are there for them as a thank you for coming to our school. Again, the subs don't always partake in the offerings, but they appreciate the offer and know it is there if they change their mind.

Chapter Eleven
Other Ideas Not Used, Yet..

I am always looking for new ways to appreciate my teachers and staff. When I hear of something, or thinking of something, I make a note of it and keep it in a file for future use. The following are ideas that are currently in that file, but I have not used them yet.

Birthday Cards for Staff from Admin

This is something I have pondered, but not actually done yet. My thought is to make a birthday card on cardstock and have one of the office ladies be over them for me. Then once a month at our weekly administrator/counselor meeting, the person over this would have everyone sign cards for the birthdays that month. After the meeting, the person over this would hang onto them and put them in the staff member's box on their birthday.

Sunglasses with "Coming Soon"

I saw this somewhere, but I don't remember where. A principal bought cheap sunglasses from somewhere like oriental trading and on the lenses wrote "Coming Soon." Then placed them in the staff boxes the week before spring break.

Sugar Scrub

Sugar scrub is super easy to make but can be costly if you use mason jars. I have seen some people use fancy Ziplock bags to save money. To make the scrub it is simply sugar, coconut oil, and essential oils. Some add a dash of food coloring to make it pretty.

Infused Water

If you have water dispensers for special occasions use them to make infused water for the staff. I actually roll this idea through my head every year. I think it would be great, but most of my staff have really big water cups or bottles they use all day. If they were to fill up their normal water cup or bottle, we would run out really fast.

Holiday Stockings

This is another idea I love, but I have not played with it yet. The idea is for every staff member to have a stocking hanging in the lounge or office hallway. The stockings would need to have teacher names on them or the teacher's name on the wall above each stocking. Then the idea is for each department to take a day and put something in the stockings.

I saw this at an elementary school. I think this would be very doable on a small campus.

Departments Take a Day of the 12 Days of Christmas

I have heard of lots of schools doing their 12 days of Christmas in this format. Luckily, I have an administrator that one of her favorite things to do is the 12 days, so she takes care of us.

Popcorn Bar

Popcorn bars can be lots of fun. I have seen them where they simply have the various flavors of salt people can add to their popcorn all the way to having candy corn, pretzels, and M&Ms you can mix with the popcorn.

Chapter Twelve

COVID

The fun that is COVID started while I was writing this book, so I decided to add a COVID section with things we have done for our staff.

Happy Hour

When the fun began in March 2020, many of my staff simply wanted to see people and socialize (we are a very social campus). With this in mind, I set up Zoom Happy Hours. They started at 4:00 since that is the end of our workday, and they were completely optional. For our first happy hour, we had over 60 people join the Zoom. It was great to see faces, catch up, and share our favorite drinks.

Goosechase

Goosechase is an online website where you can create scavenger hunts. In the early days of COVID while we were all stuck in our houses, I created a Goosechase for the staff. Each day I would add a few new missions. The missions were things they could do at their house, take a picture, and upload it. A few examples are building a toilet paper tower and what shows are you binge watching. Anyone in the Goosechase can see the pictures or typed answers from all participants. After a few days I had staff start sending me ideas for missions. They would read something like, "Mrs. Harris wants to see a picture of you reading in your favorite reading spot."

This was a fun and easy way to connect with staff. Everyone enjoyed it so much I started one for students as well.

Phone Calls

As the craziness of being at home continued, I began to worry about some of our staff who did not have family nearby. I took our staff list, added phone numbers, and then we broke the list into sections. Each administrator and counselor were assigned a section to call and check on. Then as the school shut down continued, we would rotate the list every two weeks and make phone calls. It was a great way to let the staff know we were thinking of them.

Parades

Unfortunately, one of our staff members lost his mother during the beginning of COVID. Lynn Shelton had been going to see his mom every day for about eight years. She was in a nursing home with Alzheimer's. When COVID started, he was not allowed to go see her. Then about two months into COVID, she passed away.

A former Hillwood teacher organized a parade for Lynn. Lynn has a big heart and has been there when others needed him. Close to 100 cars showed up to parade by Lynn's house to let him know we all love him.

Appreciation Time

I talked earlier about Appreciation Time where staff got jeans or sweats the next day if they participated. This time I would simply send out a Remind to the staff that said Appreciation Time and they would reach out to someone they have not talked to in a few weeks to let them know why they appreciate them.

Jib Jab

If you have not used Jib Jab to make videos for your staff, do it. It is easy and funny. So, while we were on the COVID shutdown, the week leading up to Easter, I made a Jib Jab for every day of the week and sent them out daily via Remind in the week leading up to Easter. Each day featured a different group of teachers: Fine Arts, Math, Coaches, etc.

Self Care Ideas for Stressed Out Teachers

- Blow bubbles
- Light a scented candle
- Have a relaxing cup of tea
- Write in a journal (Notebook)
- Work on a puzzle
- Make popcorn and watch a fun movie
- Celebrate the little things (Party Horn)
- "Slap" on your favorite bracelet
- Relax, we always have your back (Toy Soldier)
- Have a "Jolly" disposition
- Roll with the punches and go with the flow (Tootsie Roll)
- Go for a relaxing drive (Toy Car)
- Take time to recharge (Battery)
- Eat something healthy
- Take a walk on the sand
- Do some stretches
- Make a list of things that make you feel grateful (Postcard)
- Look through pictures that make you happy (QR Code)
- Seek out laughter... (Laffy Taffy)
- Play an instrument, sing, or dance (Kazoo)
- Color in a coloring book
- Blow off steam (Balloon)
- Stick together (HMS Car Sticker)
- Take a relaxing bath (Rubber Duck)
- Sing at the top of your lungs (Ear Plugs)
- Play a game (Game Piece)
- Have a cold one with our favorite realtors!!!

Figure 12.1: List of Items in Stress Bags

Stress Bags

Our district announced in-person instruction as opposed to remote instruction to start the year about two weeks before the teachers returned in August for their week of professional development. The announcement stressed out some staff simply due to the unknown. I recently read an article about 50 Self Care Ideas for Stress. I decided to use some of the things from the list and add in some other to create Figure 12.1.

Each thing on the list had an item for it. For instance, take a walk on the sand had a Ziplock bag of sand, do some stretches had a card with various stretches on it, have a cold one with our favorite realtors had a koozie, etc. I bought school color handle gift bags, filled them with the supplies, printed the master list on card stock, rolled it and tied it like a scroll, and put it in the bags.

The teachers were due to start back on a Monday, so the Friday before the administrators hit the road delivering bags to all of our staff. This did take a while since we had some staff that lived pretty far away, but it was well worth it!!! The staff loved getting a special delivery from an administrator.

M&Ms Heal Anything

A few years ago, someone shared with me a picture of a card that talked about how specific colors of M&Ms can help with certain "symptoms". At the end it said if you are experiencing all of the symptoms eat the whole bag. I had been wanting to do something like that for a few years, but just hadn't. I decided that with all of the fun things COVID gave us, I would use this idea to give the staff a laugh, (see Figure 12.2). Note: STAAR is the state assessment for Texas.

Teacher Appreciation Week Parent Email

Hillwood returned to in-person instruction in August 2020. Our parents had the choice of sending their student to school in-person or opting to keep their children home for remote instruction from Hillwood teachers. I kept hearing people equate reopening to building an airplane while it was in

TAKE AS DIRECTED

Red for Zooms
Blue for Forgetting Your Face Mask
for Going the Wrong Way on the Hallways
Green for Aries Issues
for STAAR
Brown for Reply Alls

If you are experiencing ALL of the above eat the whole pack!!!

Figure 12.2: M&Ms Heal Anything Card

School Transformation Through Teacher Appreciation

flight, and many times it felt that way. But by the time the first day of school rolled around, my staff was ready to rock and roll.

In October 2020, one of my assistant principals shared with me a post she had found on Facebook. Below is the post:

What it feels like to be a teacher during these COVID/Hybrid-Remote Learning times:

Imagine hosting two dinner parties at once: a BBQ in the backyard with an open fire-pit, and then the roast in the oven to be served on fine china to guests in your dining room. Now, also imagine finding time to make doggie bags for those who didn't show up. 😷

Imagine, as well, Your electric company cutting power at times briefly, where lights go off and on, and the in-house guests have to make their way back from any confusion or missed courses of the meal. Some of them joke about it. You settle them down.

Some of the dinner guests don't know how to use utensils, or clean up after themselves, are still hungry but are afraid to ask, or refuse to eat. Some complain about the food. Or claim they ate it last year. Or claim they never saw other parts of the meal before.

Some in the dining room have requested to be outside at the BBQ. Some at the BBQ now want to be in dining room. You have to keep track. Sometimes new guests arrive, sometimes guests unexpectedly leave.

The fire department might also, at any point, ask everyone to evacuate from a threat — either real or imagined. The police also expect us to huddle guests into the windowless garage, in a corner, six feet apart, in the event of an intruder — either real or imagined.

Your entire dinner party could be told at any moment to go home, and you need to quickly wrap up everyone's meals.

You do all this, while wearing a mask. While remembering to wash or sanitize hands several dozen times throughout the day. While hoping and trusting that the guests come in without any unseen illnesses brewing.

You also have to answer the phone and emails while all this is going on. Plus keep detailed records of your guests and what they ate.

The guests leave. You catch your breath. And you think about tomorrow's menu...which has to be totally different than today's.

And while you catch your breath and anxiously take inventory of ingredients for tomorrow, you know in your heart why you chose to cook for others. ♥

If you know a teacher, please take some time to reach out with a virtual hug or a note. A little kindness goes a long way. Teachers are working very hard to make sure the kids are all educated in a safe and healthy environment and meeting their social & emotional needs all when the only certainty each day is uncertainty.

Teachers are working in person, remotely and a combination of both. The day never ends."

After reading this all I could think was WOW! This is so true! I knew I wanted to share this with my parents so they could get a true idea or understanding of how amazing our teachers really are and what all they are doing for their students. If I sent this out in October 2020 it would have impacted some parents the way I hoped, but it would serve to upset some parents since we were literally still building our airplane while in flight.

I decided to hang on to it. Then the week before Teacher Appreciation Week in May, I sent it out to our parents and let them know that Teacher Appreciation Week was coming and to please show our teachers their love and appreciation. It worked so great!!! Parents got it and they went out of their way to thank teachers that week.

Trident Note

Our district lawyer, Amanda Bigbee, sent principals a pack of Trident gum with a very cute note. I decided to steal Amanda's idea. I typed the saying up on a note and had the administrators, counselors, and instructional coaches sign the note. (see Figure 12.3) After making copies of the note, I had a student tape a pack of Trident to the note and put them in staff boxes.

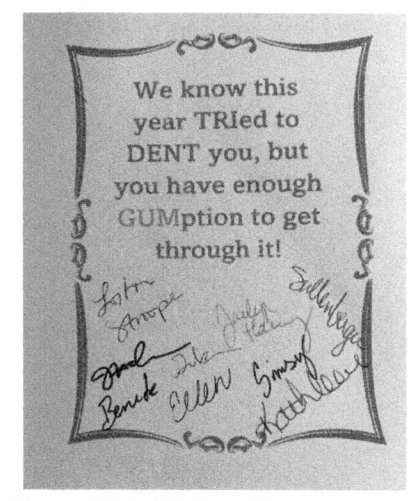

Figure 12.3: Trident Note

Conclusion

I started this book telling you that a teacher's perception is their reality. You have the power to change their perception. I hope that while reading this book you found or thought of ways you can use staff appreciation to support initiatives you have in place or initiatives you are contemplating. If not, I hope you found new ideas to show your staff how much you appreciate them.

Make the time to go visit other schools! I know we all get busy, but I have gotten so MANY ideas from simply walking around other schools.

I am always looking for new staff appreciation ideas. If you have any you would like to share, please email me Kathleen.Eckert@icloud.com and follow me on Twitter @EckertKathleen or Instagram Kathleen.Eckert

You need to have high expectations for your staff, and you have to be willing to push them out of their comfort zones. But if you back it up with support, fun, and appreciation the sky's the limit. So, how will you develop and create your campus' transformation?

Appendix

Below is a step progression of some of the initiatives discussed in this book. You cannot do everything all at once!!! When looking at and thinking about initiatives you have to look at the big picture, the impact on student achievement, and the sustainability of the initiatives before you put them into action.

As you look at the list you need to know that the items listed are automatically carried to and utilized the next year. I just did not list them out for each year because that would look very overwhelming. The only initiative from this list that we took away was Tech Badging when we no longer had a need for it, because using technology to enhance lessons and increase student achievement had become a norm for our campus.

Note: The T Chart of Campus and District initiatives from year 7 was an activity, not an initiative.

Year 1
- ☐ Open Ended Questions on Teacher Year End Survey

Year 2
- ☐ Essential Questions

Year 3
- ☐ Teachers Video Lessons
- ☐ Data Room
- ☐ Project Based Learning

Year 4
- ☐ Houses

- ☐ Professional Development Calendar (Core Content Teachers with Two Conferences)
- ☐ Husky Holla'
- ☐ Tech Badging

Year 5
- ☐ Essential Questions evolved to Essential Questions and Driving Questions
- ☐ YES (Year End Studies)

Year 6
- ☐ Home Visits in August

Year 7
- ☐ T Chart Campus and District Initiatives

Year 8
- ☐ Husky Holla' evolved to ICE (Investigating Classroom Excellence)

Year 9
- ☐ COVID
- ☐ Project Based Learning evolved to Workshop Based Learning

Made in United States
North Haven, CT
27 February 2022